BOOK G
READING FOR CONCEPTS

"Learning without thought is labor lost." Confucius

BOOK G
READING

FOR CONCEPTS
Third Edition

Phoenix Learning Resources
New York

Reading for Concepts
Third Edition
Book G

Contributing Authors for the Reading for Concepts Series

Linda Barton, feature writer for *St. Louis Today*
Roberta H. Berry, elementary school teacher, writer
Barbara Broeking, journalist and educational publications editor
Eth Clifford, author of many volumes of fiction and poetry for youth
Ellen Dolan, juvenile book author
Barbara R. Frey, Professor of Education, State University College, Buffalo, N.Y.
Ruth Harley, author and editor of young people's periodicals
Andrew Kaplan, content–area reading specialist
Phyllis W. Kirk, children's book editor
Richard Kirk, author of science, social studies, and reading books for youth
Thomas D. Mantel, attorney and juvenile author
Marilyn F. Peachin, journalist and editor
James N. Rogers, author-editor of science and social studies resource books
James J. Pflaum, author and editor of current events periodicals
Gloria S. Rosenzweig, writer of children's books
Jean Shirley, author of juvenile books
Rosemary Winebrenner, editor of children's books
Jean White, journalist and writer of young people's reference materials

Vocabulary
Cynthia Merman, Reading and Language Specialist

Project Management and Production
Kane Publishing Services, Inc.

Cover Design
Pencil Point Studios

Text Design
Jim Darby

Illustrators
James Cummings; Linda S. Pierce; Al Pucci, GAI

ISBN 0–7915–2109-5

3 4 5 6 7 8 9 0 05 04

TABLE OF CONTENTS

TO THE TEACHER

Purpose

This book is one of eight in the series "Reading for Concepts." It was designed to provide an opportunity for young readers to grow in reading experience while exploring a wide variety of ideas contained in the major academic disciplines.

Four basic underlying concepts are reflected in this book. They are: *Some things are not what they seem; People's ideas about things change from time to time; The same ideas are seen in different ways by different groups;* and *Similar things are changing all over the world at different rates.* The overriding concept in this book is perspective and contrasting views and viewpoints. To illustrate these concepts, stories have been written around intriguing pieces of information that reflect these ideas. Content has been drawn from disciplines of history, art, biology, economics, Earth science, space, political science, engineering, anthropology, and geography. In this way, a wide array of content for meeting various interests has been assured.

A narrative follows stories 20, 40, and 60. The narratives, largely drawn from folk literature, will provide a change of pace and are "just for fun" types of stories.

Teaching Procedure

Detailed suggestions for presenting the selections in this book will be found on pages 15 and 16 in the Teacher's Guide. Difficult words, with grade-level definitions, are listed by story on pages 6-12. Important content-area proper nouns not defined in the text are included in this listing.

Following each article is a test, which is especially designed to improve specific skills in reading. The test items were created to incorporate the thinking skills reflected in Benjamin S. Bloom's *Taxonomy of Educational Objectives*, which is explained on pages 6-7 in the Teacher's Guide.

Concept Recapitulations

After students have completed each of the three sections of this book, you may conduct a discussion to tie together the information carried in the individual articles in terms of the overall concept. Guiding questions are found on page 13 for Concept I, page 57 for Concept II, page 101 for Concept III, and page 145 for Concept IV.

Have a few priming possibilities ready to suggest, or shape them out of earlier offerings from the group. Sophisticated statements and a review of specifics are not to be expected. Look for signs of mental play and the movement of information from one setting to another. It is perfectly reasonable to conclude with unanswered questions for students to ponder in retrospect. However, it is important to give students the satisfaction of enthusiastic acceptance of their early attempts at this type of open-ended speculation.

STEPS FOR THE READER

A. Turn to page 14. Look at the picture. Read the title. Think about what the story will say.

B. Study the words for this page on the list beginning on page 6.

C. Read the story carefully.

D. Put your name and the title of the story on a sheet of paper.

   Number from one to nine. Begin the test on the page next to the story.

   1. This question asks you to remember something the story has told you. Which of the four choices is correct for this sentence?

   2. The question asks you to find the word in the story that means the same as the words in italics. The question gives you a paragraph number. Read that part again to be sure you have the right word.

   3. Reread the paragraph given. Which word is described by the words given in the question? The given words must modify or explain the word or words you select.

   4. This question wants you to think about the story. The answer is not in your book. Read the choices. Choose the one that is the very best guess you might make from the ideas you have just read.

   5. The question tests your memory for a detail. Which of the choices agrees with the story?

   6. This question asks you to choose a statement about the entire story. Don't select an idea that fits only one small part. Your answer should fit all of the story.

   7. On the basis of the story, which of the choices is most likely to be true? The answer is not in the story. You will have to think about the ideas and draw your own conclusions.

   8. Questions 8 asks why. You must select the best explanation from those listed. The cause should be the one given in the article.

   9. Question 9 asks you to think about the article in relation to the concept for the group of articles. The statement you select must be true for the article. It should also be a good illustration of the concept in action.

E. Check your work. The answers for the first test are given below. Your teacher may let you use the answer key for other tests. She or he may check your work for you.

F. Put the number correct at the top of your paper. Now go back and recheck the answers that were wrong. Do you see now how the correct answer was better? How can you get ready to do the next test better?

G. Turn to page 186. The directions tell you how to put your score onto a record chart. Your teacher will tell you if you may write in the book. If not, he or she will help you make a copy for your notebook.

Looking for the Big Idea

The next page asks questions about the big ideas in this book. Read the page and think about the ideas.

Just for Fun

Your book has three longer stories that are just for fun. These stories, beginning on pages 54, 98, and 142, are from old folktales. There are no questions to answer.

Answers for Practice Test, page 15		
1. b	2. conquer	3. wooden horse
4. a	5. a	6. b
7. c	8. a	9. c

Vocabulary Words and Definitions

PAGE 14
disguise hide; make something look different
priest a religious leader
Sparta a city in ancient Greece
Troy a city in ancient Turkey

PAGE 16
constantly all the time; not stopping
effect the idea that something is happening
exhausted very tired
fording going through water
notion idea
resourceful with many good ideas

PAGE 18
crustaceans (krəs tā´shənz) shellfish
dense close together
streamers ribbons
stubby short
vast very large

PAGE 20
imitates acts like something else
larva baby insects that look like worms
mimic something that pretends to be something else
predators animals that eat other animals; enemies
resembles looks like
species a group of the same kind of animal; for example, collies and poodles are both members of the dog species
wingspread distance from the end of one wing to the end of the other

PAGE 22
article a thing; item
dramatic exciting; fun
sacrifice loss
tourists visitors from another place; travelers

PAGE 24
accustomed used to
cubic relating to volume, the amount a container holds
established decided on
standards rules

PAGE 26
coined made up a word

PAGE 26 continued
descendants the people who come after you; children and grandchildren are descendants
refer to call by a name; describe
resident a person who lives in a certain place

PAGE 28
fanciful made up; hard to believe
furthermore also; too
gullible easy to fool
phrases expressions; groups of words
scorn dislike; disrespect
seafaring having to do with sailors and ships
wrestled fought; boxed

PAGE 30
experienced skillful
image a picture; not the real thing
mirage something that isn't really there
refraction bending of light rays
regretfully sadly

PAGE 32
atmosphere air
elevated up in the air; off the ground
enabled made something happen

PAGE 34
desperately as if your life depends on it
doomed sure to die
mass a lot of something
subsurface water a little way under the ground
temporarily for a few moments
treacherous dangerous

PAGE 36
anti-apartheid (an tī ə pär´tāt) against South Africa's old policy of racial segregation
choreographer someone who creates dances
founded began an institution
grace beauty
jealousy wanting something that someone else has
represent tell the story of; use movements to suggest words
transformed changed

PAGE 38
constellations groups of stars
simultaneously at the same time

PAGE 40
disk circle

6

PAGE 40 continued
focus look at; see clearly
unaccustomed new and different

PAGE 42
distributed gave away
envious jealous; wanting what someone else has
generation people living at the same time
resented disliked
ridiculed made fun of
steward the person who manages a household

PAGE 44
ceased stopped
charter a written list of rights and laws
constitutional according to a written list of rights and laws
coronation crowning someone queen or king
legislative lawmaking
restored got power again

PAGE 46
absolutely 100 percent
architects people who decide how buildings will look
illusion something that looks different from the way it really is
optical with the eyes

PAGE 48
studios rooms where people work
vapor smoke

PAGE 50
artificial made by people, not found in nature
billiard ball a ball used in billiards, a game where you hit balls with a stick to make them go into pockets in a table
camphor chemical made from the bark of the camphor tree
cellophane thin paper you can see through
developed invented

PAGE 52
cast iron a very strong metal
exerts pushes
quality ability; a characteristic
rigid stiff; not able to move
stress pressure; force
suspension held up by support at the top, instead of by legs underneath

PAGE 52 continued
welded heated pieces of metal so that they stick together

PAGES 54–56
heaved threw
Norse from Norway
quivered moved
resolved decided
structure a building
triumphantly having won
trough (trôf) a big container for food
wager a bet

PAGE 58
accompany to go along with
claimed took as one's own
severely strongly; strictly

PAGE 60
theory idea

PAGE 62
ornamental pretty but not useful
varieties different kinds

PAGE 64
complex made of many parts
generation birth
microscopic too small to be seen
preserve keep fresh
spontaneous happening naturally

PAGE 66
per for each
profitable making money
resentment anger

PAGE 68
ebony black wood
latex liquid rubber
thriving successful

PAGE 70
cultured high-class and educated
profession job; career
respectable proper; allowed
strictly only

PAGE 72
grinders machines that turn coffee beans into powder
merchandise things for sale
mink an expensive fur

PAGE 74
cellulose material from plants that is used to make paper
exiles people who are not allowed to go home
technicians people who study and work with machines

PAGE 76
affected changed
maintaining keeping the same
seep drip

PAGE 78
archbishop a powerful man in the church
Babylonians people who lived in Babylonia in the ancient Middle East
geologists scientists who study Earth
ranges strings of mountains
scholars educated people; thinkers

PAGE 80
according to depending on
archeologists scientists who study old civilizations
classified organized
minerals stones; rocks
naturalists people who study nature
upheaval big change

PAGE 82
altered changed
carbon an element
elements basic parts
philosopher a person who thinks about why things happen
substance what something is made of

PAGE 84
astronomer someone who studies stars and planets
molten fiery rock
observations studies
probes studies

PAGE 86
compete to try to do better than someone else
hurdling jumping over fences

PAGE 86 continued
javelin a long spear
Olympics a series of athletic events that began in ancient Greece thousands of years ago and continues today

PAGE 88
captives prisoners
existed has been
opinion people's thoughts
Quakers a religious group

PAGE 90
ballads songs that tell stories
classical music of the 18th and 19th centuries in Europe
descent ancestors; heritage
spirituals religious songs
symphony a long musical work for an orchestra

PAGE 92
agriculture plants
flourished grew a lot of plants

PAGE 94
attitudes beliefs; ways of thinking
barbed with sharp points
privilege favor
tiller part of an old kind of car (or boat) that helps it change direction

PAGE 96
energy the source of movement
illuminating gas gas that was used in street lamps to provide light
internal-combustion heat to power the car is made inside the engine
self-propelled moving itself with a source of energy onboard
undependable didn't always work properly

PAGES 98–100
assume pretend to be something else
grimly seriously
mischievous playful and tricky
offended angry
pursuing following
raging angry
shattered broken

PAGE 102
homesteaders people who moved west to live and farm
nesters the nickname for homesteaders
range flat land without many trees
subdued killed or silenced

PAGE 104
disuse not being used anymore
enthusiastic happy; having energy
idle not being used
navigable big enough for ships to sail on
prosperity wealth; money
superior better
system many parts connected together

PAGE 106
absorbed taken into
algae water plants, like seaweed
biology the study of living things
botanists scientists who study plants
category a group
chlorophyll material that makes plants green
classification a label
organism a living thing
protozoans tiny animals with only one cell
stagnant water that does not move
zoologists scientists who study animals

PAGE 108
arteries vessels that carry blood away from the heart
central middle
circulated traveled through the body
contraction a squeezing
expansion getting bigger
oozed dripped
opposed disagreed with
veins vessels that carry blood toward the heart
vital necessary for life

PAGE 110
compact small
economical less expensive
export sell in other countries
midsize not big and not small
mileage how many miles a car can travel on a gallon of gas
minivan small van
preferences what people like best
shortages lacks; not enough of
utility use

PAGE 112
hoard a large collection of something
imprisonment being put in jail
incredible so big that it is unbelievable
secure to buy
wrought shaped

PAGE 114
anthropologists people who study how people live
authority power and importance
civilizations groups of people
designer someone who makes clothes
donned wore; put on
headgear hats, crowns, and other things worn on the head
Orient Asia
reputation what people think about someone
status one's place in society
symbolizes shows; gives a picture of

PAGE 116
associated connected with
delicacy a treat
determines decides; causes
llama an animal related to a camel that lives in the mountains of South America
Orthodox the most religious Jewish people
vegetarians people who do not eat meat
yaks big, furry animals like oxen

PAGE 118
adapt change
European-type animals that are native to Europe
processed made into food
wildebeest (wil′dǝ bēst) a large African animal; a gnu

PAGE 120
barren where nothing grows
converted changed
expose to uncover or reveal
federal the national government
generating making
pastures fields of grass for animals to use
process action; something that is happening
ridges small hills
subsoil the lower layer of soil
unfilled empty

PAGE 122
fossil part of an animal or plant that was buried millions of years ago
glacial having to do with glaciers (sheets of ice)
observed watched
unsorted all mixed up together

PAGE 124
arguments disagreements
geology the study of Earth
granite a hard rock
receded got shallower; moved back
underworld the place where the souls of dead people go

PAGE 126
carbon dioxide a gas that is in air
collided bumped into each other
comet an object in space that has a long tail
core center
meteors small pieces of matter in outer space
nucleus the important central part of something
orbit the path of or around a planet
particles little bits and pieces
prediction a guess about what will happen in the future

PAGE 128
admit agree
constant steady; not stopping
galaxies groups of many stars

PAGE 130
in spite of no matter that
issue subject

PAGE 132
acceptable liked; approved of
individual each; alone
legislature a group of people who make laws
represented stood for; the number of people from their states who would go to Congress

PAGE 134
cathedral a large church
commandment a law made by God
emblems shapes used in place of something else
graven images idols; pictures of people or animals to be worshiped
mosaics pictures made with small pieces of colored stones

PAGE 134 continued
portrayed showed
stained colored
symbolized used a picture of one thing to mean something else
synagogues Jewish temples

PAGE 136
colleagues people working at the same job
congressional in the Congress of the United States
equality everyone treated the same
mainland the United States
sponsored wrote
tariffs taxes on goods from other countries
tourism people visiting a place on vacation

PAGE 138
awkward big and hard to hold
ornately with a lot of designs
pry to break open; push or pull
purpose a use
tampered used without permission

PAGE 140
automated powered by electricity; not using people
concourses open spaces inside buildings
international going between different countries
primary first; most important
remote far-away
terminal a building for planes, buses, trains and their passengers

PAGES 142–144
brilliance shine; a bright light
droop get weak and fall over
gracious kind and polite
grants agrees to
sow to plant seeds
spun made thread
timid shy and quiet
withered curled up and died

PAGE 146
assemblies small groups of people in government
campaign to work toward a goal
Muslim believing in the religion of Islam
nonviolent peaceful
struggle hard work

PAGE 148
dependent ruled by another country
emerging beginning; coming out
empires the lands owned by one country
independent free; self-governing
territory area
tolerate accept; agree to

PAGE 150
biologists the scientists who study living things
common usual; a lot of
hereditary passed from parents to children
industrial with many factories
lichens (lī´kə̄nz) small plants that grow on rocks and
    trees
mutation a biological change
preyed eaten by
readily often; easily
survival ability to live

PAGE 152
commercial business; to sell for a profit
exhaust use up
oxygen air
plagued bothered
plankton tiny plants and animals in the ocean
secretion something produced inside a plant or animal

PAGE 154
acre a small area of land
cyanide (sī´ə nīd) a poison
droughts times when there is no rain
Eritrea a country in east Africa
process make useful
productive able to grow a lot of crops
resist protected from harm
solution the answer
techniques methods; ways of doing something

PAGE 156
funds money
medieval during the Middle Ages (500–1500) in
    Europe
motion movement
network many things connected together
sensors machines that can sense movement
technology the science of machines
terminal the keyboard and monitor of a computer
transfer to move from one place to another
withdraw to take out

PAGE 158
catalytic converter the part of a car that changes
    poisonous gases into water and harmless gases
exhausts gases that come out of a car or plane
thermal inversions when the air close to the ground
    is cooler than the air just above
toxic poisonous

PAGE 160
Aboriginal describing the Aborigines, the first people
    to live in Australia
campuses colleges
compose to write; create
outback areas very far away from cities
short-wave radio a kind of radio that is like a
    telephone
traditional usual
virtual like the real thing

PAGE 162
cubic length times width times height; like a cube
evaporates turns into air
levees hills of earth at the sides of rivers to prevent
    flooding

PAGE 164
access open to the people
independent separate; owned by individuals
opinions ideas; beliefs
receivers machines that get sounds and pictures that
    people can look at
satellite a machine orbiting Earth that can send
    sounds and pictures from one place to another

PAGE 166
aloft up in the air
altitudes distances from the ground
comparable similar
currents moving air
existence reality
hemisphere half of Earth above (north) or below
    (south) the equator
startling surprising
velocity speed

PAGE 168
amphibian an animal such as a frog, toad, or
    salamander
imbedded buried
mantle the layer of earth just below the crust (top
    layer)

meteorologist a scientist who studies weather and climate
sandstone a soft kind of stone

PAGE 170
astronomers scientists who study stars and planets
brilliant bright
emitted gave off
nebula a cloud in outer space
nova a star that suddenly gets very bright
supernova an exploding star
visible able to be seen

PAGE 172
executives people who run businesses
exhibits pictures and other things
historic very important
investor someone who buys stock in a company
opportunity a chance
stock brokerage a business that sells shares of stock in companies to individuals
subsidiaries small companies that are part of a larger company

PAGE 174
absolute total
candidate a person running for an office
Conservative Party a political party in England
dictator someone who takes over a country without being elected
dictatorship a government ruled by one person who is not elected
free elections where people may vote privately for whomever they choose; democratic governments hold free elections
Labor Party a political party in England
multi-party having many political parties

PAGE 176
ballots votes
bore contained; showed
computerized using computers
Middle Ages the years 500 to 1500 in Europe
yoked chained to a plow

PAGE 178
alternating on and off; starting and stopping
circuits wires that go in a circle
commercials advertisements on radio and TV

PAGE 178 continued
devices machines
electro-magnetic using electricity and magnetism
electronic operated by means of a computer
range series; from first to last
telharmonium a musical instrument like an electric piano
theremin (ther´∂ m∂n) a musical instrument that uses moving air to make sounds

PAGE 180
contemporary modern; today
oriental from the Orient, or Asia
primitive not new or modern
specialty the main attraction
specific only one
Tokyo the capital of the Asian nation Japan
viewers people who are watching something

PAGE 182
considerations factors; things people think are important
constructed built
corrugated bumpy
designers artists
mesh wires with spaces in between, like a window screen
polyester a kind of plastic
popular liked by many people; widespread
variety many different kinds

PAGE 184
cooperative (kō ä´pr∂ tiv) sharing
communes groups of people living together and sharing the work
immigrants people who move from one country to another to live
residents people who live in the same place
Soviet Union the former name of Russia and its allied nations
Swedish things relating to the European nation Sweden
trade school a high school in which people learn job skills

I

Some Things Are Not What They Seem

In this section, you will read about many things that are not what they first seemed to be. You will read about these things in the areas of history, biology, economics, anthropology, geography, Earth science, space, political science, art and engineering.

Keep these questions in mind when you are reading.

1. What are some things that are not what they seem to be?

2. What leads us to be fooled?

3. What can we do to find out the truth about something?

4. Is it always possible to find the truth?

5. If it is not always possible to uncover the truth, what do we then do?

Look on pages 6-7 for help with words you don't understand in this section.

The Horse That Won a War

To camouflage something means to disguise it. From the ancient Greeks comes a legend of a camouflage so successful that it won a war!

The Trojan War began with the kidnapping of a beautiful woman. Paris, the son of the King of Troy, fell in love with Helen, wife of the King of Sparta. He kidnapped Helen and brought her to his home in Troy. The angry Greeks decided to bring Helen home and destroy Troy. For ten long, hard years, Trojans fought Greeks outside the walls of Troy, but neither side was able to conquer the other.

At last, a Greek leader thought of a way to get inside the strong Trojan walls. He ordered a huge and hollow wooden horse to be built. The horse was so tremendous that it could easily hold 100 Greek soldiers. The wooden animal, with soldiers hidden inside, was placed outside the walls of Troy. The Greeks then made a big show of leaving Troy and sailing off in their ships.

The Trojans, seeing the Greeks leave, flung open the gates of their city and crowded around the great wooden horse. A wise priest warned that it was a trick, but the curious Trojans moved the horse inside the gates. They insisted it was not a trick. With their own eyes they had seen the Greeks depart.

That night, while the Trojans celebrated their seeming victory, a Greek prisoner managed to reach the horse and open a hidden door in its side. The Greek soldiers slipped quietly out of their hiding place, opened the gates of Troy, and signaled the Greek ships.

The city of Troy fell that night to the clever Greeks.

FIND THE ANSWERS

1. A Greek leader thought of a way to
    a. trick a priest. c. talk to the Trojans.
    b. get inside the Trojan walls. d. build a wooden gate.

2. The word in paragraph 2 that means *overcome by force* is _____.

3. The words "that it could easily hold 100 Greek soldiers" in paragraph 3 refer to the _____ _____.

4. While it is not directly stated, the article suggests that
    a. cleverness can be more important than strength.
    b. everything that happened was Helen's fault.
    c. most wars last at least ten years or more.

5. The wooden horse was placed
    a. outside the walls of Troy.
    b. inside the Trojan ships.
    c. outside the gates of Greece.

6. On the whole, the article tells about
    a. signals used on Greek ships.
    b. the trick that captured Troy.
    c. a prince and a beautiful woman.

7. Which statement does the article lead you to believe?
    a. The Trojans could not see very well.
    b. Greek prisoners always hide in horses.
    c. The Trojan priest could have saved Troy.

8. Why did the Greek leader use a trick to get into Troy?
    a. He wanted the long, hard war to come to an end.
    b. He wanted to see how many men would fit into a horse.
    c. He wanted to keep his soldiers busy with work.

9. Think about the concept for this group of articles. Which statement seems true both for the article and for the concept?
    a. You can't fool people with tricks.
    b. People should not be curious.
    c. We cannot always believe what we see.

The Mighty Army

On February 23, 1779, a ragged group of men were approaching a fort held by British soldiers in Vincennes, Indiana. The men were Americans. Their leader was a man named George Rogers Clark. Clark and his small army of about 125 men were determined to capture the fort. To accomplish this task, they had marched across Illinois through mud and rain, fording dangerously swollen rivers on foot and by canoe.

The men were exhausted. They had almost no ammunition. By the time they neared Vincennes, they had been without food for two days. Yet before they could attack the fort, they had to capture the town. Clark, a daring and resourceful man, sent a message to the townspeople. In it, Clark advised townspeople who were for the British to go to the fort immediately. All others were to stay inside their homes. His army, Clark's message warned, was big and powerful!

To convince the townspeople that this was so, Clark made his weary men march in and out of the hills around Vincennes. They marched from early afternoon until dark to give the townspeople the notion that Clark's army was so big it took that much time for all the men to reach Vincennes. Some men, on Clark's orders, also carried flags on long poles so that the banners were constantly visible in the town.

The townspeople thought Clark's army was a mighty one indeed! The town fell to Clark and his men and not a shot was fired. Clark and his men created the effect of a furious battle outside the fort. On February 25, the fort, which had enough supplies to hold out another six months, surrendered to the ragged American army!

1. George Rogers Clark had an army of about
   - a. 2,000 men.
   - c. 125 men.
   - b. 900 men.
   - d. 400 men.

2. The word in paragraph 4 that means *gave up* is

   _____ .

3. The words "a daring and resourceful man" in paragraph 2 describe

   _____ .

4. While it is not directly stated, the article suggests that
   - a. Illinois is always full of mud and rain.
   - b. Clark was a great leader and hero to his men.
   - c. it is not a good idea to put flags on long poles.

5. The fort had enough supplies to hold out
   - a. one more year.
   - b. at least ten days.
   - c. another six months.

6. On the whole, the article tells about
   - a. the capture of a fort against great odds.
   - b. the townspeople in Vincennes, Indiana.
   - c. an army that carried visible banners.

7. Which statement does the article lead you to believe?
   - a. Crossing a swollen river on foot is a lot of fun.
   - b. All mighty armies are made up of 125 ragged men.
   - c. Most townspeople wanted Clark's men to take the fort.

8. Why did the people in the fort surrender to Clark?
   - a. They thought the townspeople wanted this.
   - b. They thought they were fighting a large army.
   - c. They didn't want to stay in Indiana anymore.

9. Think about the concept for this group of articles. Which statement seems true both for the article and for the concept?
   - a. Men fight better when they are exhausted and hungry.
   - b. Noise and confusion can make a few seem like many.
   - c. Clark and his men stayed inside the houses in town.

Strange Fish in a Strange Sea

There is a fish that does not look like a fish, which lives in a sea that is not a sea. The fish is the sargassum fish, sometimes called a "fishing frog." The sea is the Sargasso Sea, a vast tangle of floating seaweed in the middle of the Atlantic Ocean. This seaweed is known as sargassum.

The sargassum fish looks like a small handful of seaweed. Its body is covered with knobs and streamers that look like trailing plants. The fish's greenish-brown coloring can change a little to match the color of the weeds around it.

The sargassum fish is about 1½ inches long. This tiny fish is a poor swimmer. It uses its stubby fins almost like legs to creep through the dense tangle of plants. Most of the time it remains quietly in one place. It is so nearly invisible among the plants that it is safe from its enemies.

The sargassum fish waits in hiding for the small fish and crustaceans that it eats. When one of these small creatures is near, the sargassum fish suddenly opens its mouth and water rushes in, carrying along a tiny victim with it. The sargassum fish is a greedy eater, and spends much of its time on the lookout for food.

The Sargasso Sea is not the only place in which sargassum seaweed grows. This seaweed is also found floating in the Gulf Stream, and in the western part of the Pacific Ocean. Wherever this weed is found, the sargassum fish is likely to be hiding there, too.

1. The sargassum fish is
    a. a poor swimmer.   c. a handful of seaweed.
    b. a small frog.   d. always invisible.

2. The word in paragraph 3 that means *short and thick* is _____.

3. The words "a vast tangle of floating seaweed" in paragraph 1

    describe the _____ _____.

4. While it is not directly stated, the article suggests that
    a. camouflage often saves the sargassum fish's life.
    b. these fish are the most beautiful fish in the sea.
    c. fish would live longer if they could not swim.

5. The sargassum fish is about
    a. 10 inches deep.
    b. 2 feet wide.
    c. 1½ inches long.

6. On the whole, the article tells about
    a. the lures fishers use to catch the sargassum fish.
    b. the kind of plants found in the Sargasso Sea.
    c. the life and habits of the sargassum fish.

7. Which statement does the article lead you to believe?
    a. Fish look better when they appear to be weeds.
    b. The sargassum fish is found everywhere in the world.
    c. The sargassum fish is prey for larger fish.

8. Why does the sargassum fish use its fins almost like legs?
    a. It enjoys walking.
    b. It is a poor swimmer.
    c. It is too big to swim.

9. Think about the concept for this group of articles. Which statement seems true
    both for the article and for the concept?
    a. A fish may be mistaken for a plant.
    b. All fish are very fussy eaters.
    c. Most weeds grow in the Sargasso Sea.

The Model and the Mimic

Two brightly colored butterflies have just flown by. They appear to be exactly alike, but actually one is a little larger than the other. The larger insect has a wingspread of up to four inches. The smaller one has a wingspread of less than three inches. The smaller butterfly also has an extra black line on its rear wings.

At first glance, it is hard to tell them apart. Would you guess from this that they are different-sized butterflies of the same species? Or that they are different species of butterflies but close relatives belonging to the same family? If you said yes to either question, you would be wrong, for these look-alikes belong to quite different families.

The larger insect is the monarch butterfly. In its larva stage, the monarch feeds on milkweed, which seems to give the monarch a disagreeable taste and smell. The bright coloring of the monarch acts as a warning sign to predators. Birds that eat butterflies soon recognize the monarch and quickly learn to leave it alone.

The smaller insect is the viceroy, which feeds on the leaves of aspen, poplar, and willow trees in its larva stage. Birds would find this insect tasty, but because it resembles the monarch, birds avoid it. The viceroy's resemblance to the monarch gives it some protection from its enemies and helps it survive.

There are other pairs of look-alike butterflies, moths, bees, and wasps. In each case, one either has a disagreeable taste or odor, or can give a painful sting. This one is called the model. The insect that imitates this model for protection is called the mimic.

FIND THE ANSWERS

1. The bright coloring of the monarch warns away
   - a. butterflies.
   - b. small insects.
   - c. the mimics.
   - d. predators.

2. The word in paragraph 3 that means *know again* is _____.

3. The words "a disagreeable taste and smell" in paragraph 3 refer to the

   _____.

4. While it is not directly stated, the article suggests that
   - a. birds don't know too much about insects.
   - b. butterflies have a lot of relatives.
   - c. imitation is another kind of camouflage.

5. The rear wings of the viceroy have
   - a. a wide colored line.
   - b. an extra black line.
   - c. five extra red dots.

6. On the whole, the article tells about
   - a. the taste and smell of milkweed.
   - b. a monarch who rules the butterflies.
   - c. look-alikes in the insect world.

7. Which statement does the article lead you to believe?
   - a. There are not many look-alikes among insects.
   - b. Insects do not feed on the same kinds of plants.
   - c. There is only one species of butterfly.

8. Why is the viceroy able to survive?
   - a. Its resemblance to the monarch gives it protection.
   - b. Its resemblance to the larva helps it stay alive.
   - c. Its appearance on the willow tree protects it.

9. Think about the concept for this group of articles. Which statement seems true both for the article and for the concept?
   - a. Different-sized butterflies attack large birds.
   - b. The eye is not always quick to see differences.
   - c. The viceroy butterfly eats too much milkweed.

The Price Nobody Pays

In the villages of Mexico, as in some other parts of the world, shopping is a kind of game. In the fine department stores, of course, buyers pay the prices listed on the tags. But in most villages, bargaining is a dramatic game both buyers and sellers enjoy.

Suppose a merchant is a Mexican shopkeeper who sells handmade silver jewelry to tourists. Among the items of jewelry is a pair of earrings a tourist wants to buy. The merchant names a price. Immediately the tourist makes a much lower offer. The price the merchant puts on an article is not usually the price which will finally be paid. But the merchant pretends to be shocked. The tourist is told that the earrings are real silver, made by people who live in the mountains. It takes a long time to make such remarkable ear-

rings. But at great sacrifice the merchant will let the tourist have the earrings at a lower price. The two bargain. The tourist comes up a little, the merchant comes down a little. At last they agree on what both consider to be a fair price.

While the two bargain, they speak of other things as well. The merchant may gossip about life in the village or mention interesting sights the tourist should see before leaving Mexico.

The merchant's way of doing business is much older than the supermarket way. It dates back to Old World times when the town market was the only place where people could exchange news and visit with friends. Bargaining made their lives a little more colorful.

In Mexico today, bargaining still makes life colorful for some merchants.

FIND THE ANSWERS

1. The way a Mexican merchant runs a business is
   - a. faster than ours.
   - b. an old way.
   - c. a new way.
   - d. like a supermarket.

2. The word in paragraph 2 that means *think of* or *regard as* is

   _____ .

3. The words "where people could exchange news and visit with friends" in

   paragraph 4 describe the town _____ .

4. While it is not directly stated, the article suggests that
   - a. one cannot be sure of the real price of some things.
   - b. merchants in Mexico would rather talk than sell things.
   - c. tourists do not enjoy bargaining for silver earrings.

5. The town market was once the only place where
   - a. people could visit with friends.
   - b. people could find fine department stores.
   - c. people could fight with enemies.

6. On the whole, the article tells about
   - a. tourists who go to town markets.
   - b. craftspeople who live in mountains.
   - c. bargaining in villages in Mexico.

7. Which statement does the article lead you to believe?
   - a. All jewelry in Mexico costs too much money.
   - b. Tourists who travel in Mexico are never fair.
   - c. This kind of shopping can be fun for tourists.

8. Why is bargaining often carried on in the villages?
   - a. It helps the people see interesting sights.
   - b. It helps make the people's lives more colorful.
   - c. It proves that jewelry can be made of silver.

9. Think about the concept for this group of articles. Which statement seems true
   both for the article and for the concept?
   - a. The first price you hear may not be the real one.
   - b. Gossip is more important than money.
   - c. No one in Mexico will bargain with you.

When Is a Gallon Not a Gallon?

A long time ago, when ancient Rome was still an empire, people of that time used similar weights and measures. The standards for these weights and measures were established by the Romans, who kept these standards in a temple in Rome. All standards for measuring weight or distance were the same, whether in Spain or in Syria. But then the Roman Empire fell, and these standards disappeared. Today, standards vary from place to place throughout the world.

Tourists who drive from the United States into Canada, for example, are surprised when they buy gasoline for their cars. A gallon of gas costs more than they are accustomed to paying. They complain that prices are much higher in Canada than in the United States. Then they discover that they can drive farther on a Canadian gallon than on a United States gallon.

Is it a different kind of gas? No, it is a different kind of gallon. Canada uses the British, or imperial, gallon that is about one-fifth larger than the United States gallon.

Four quarts equal a gallon and two pints equal a quart in both countries. But Canada's quarts and pints are larger than quarts and pints in the United States. The imperial gallon equals 277.42 cubic inches while the gallon in the United States is equal to 231 cubic inches. Measured in ounces, Canada's large gallon holds 160 fluid ounces, while the smaller United States gallon holds no more than 128 fluid ounces. From these figures, it is easy to see why Americans can drive farther on the Canadian gallon than on the American gallon.

Someday, countries may follow the example of the ancient Romans and make weights and measures the same for every nation.

IMPERIAL GALLON

AMERICAN GALLON

FIND THE ANSWERS

1. Canada has a different kind of
   - a. gasoline.
   - b. gallon.
   - c. tourist.
   - d. driver.

2. The word in paragraph 2 that means *find fault* or *express annoyance* is

   _____ .

3. The words "that is about one-fifth larger than the United States gallon" in

   paragraph 3 describe the British or imperial _____ .

4. While it is not directly stated, the article suggests that
   - a. too many tourists now go to Canada.
   - b. different measures can be a problem.
   - c. the United States cannot measure an ounce.

5. A gallon of gas in Canada costs more
   - a. than Americans are used to paying.
   - b. than the ancient Romans charged.
   - c. than the imperial British like.

6. On the whole, the article tells about
   - a. the gallon in the United States and Canada.
   - b. cubic inches in the Roman Empire.
   - c. surprised tourists in Canada.

7. Which statement does the article lead you to believe?
   - a. Americans should not travel so much.
   - b. No one in Rome ever went to a temple.
   - c. It would be good to use the same measures everywhere.

8. Why are American tourists surprised?
   - a. The price of a Canadian gallon of gas seems high.
   - b. They didn't know Canada sold gasoline.
   - c. They weigh more in Canada than in the United States.

9. Think about the concept for this group of articles. Which statement seems true
   both for the article and for the concept?
   - a. Americans are always complaining about gas.
   - b. The same name may mean two different things.
   - c. Ancient Rome fell because of poor standards.

Hoosier or Gander

Is the naming of places or peoples intentional or accidental? Sometimes it is the first, but very often it is the second!

American Indians got their name from Columbus, who happened upon the West Indies and Central America in his search for India. He called the people of these lands *Indios* because he thought they were natives of India. Columbus wrote about his voyages in Spanish, but when his writings were translated into English, the word *Indios* became *Indians.* It was the wrong name for people not native to India, and descendants of these original settlers are now often known as Native Americans.

We refer to people in some of our states by special names. In Indiana, they are known as *Hoosiers.* People from Michigan call themselves *Michiganders.* The word *Michigander* was coined in the year 1848 as a joke about a man who wanted to be president of the United States. The man was General Lewis Cass. People opposing him poked fun at him, saying that the word *Cass* meant *goose.* They began to call him the gander from Michigan, or the Michigander. In later years, the original use of the word was forgotten, and the name came to mean any resident of Michigan.

It is not known why Indiana became the Hoosier State. Does *Hoosier* come from the ancient Saxon word *hoozer*? In England, a hoozer was someone who lived in the hills. Some people insist Hoosier came from the familiar pioneer greeting, "Who's yere?"

What are the people of your state called? Do you know how your state came by its name, or what the name means?

FIND THE ANSWERS

1. In Indiana, the people are called
   - a. Indians.
   - b. Hawaiians.
   - c. Hopis.
   - d. Hoosiers.

2. The word in paragraph 3 that means *made up* is _____.

3. The words "from the ancient Saxon word *hoozer*" in paragraph 4 describe
   _____.

4. While it is not directly stated, the article suggests that
   - a. the Native Americans asked Columbus to give them a name.
   - b. people do not know how some words began.
   - c. General Cass raised ganders in Michigan.

5. Columbus wrote about his voyages in
   - a. English.
   - b. Italian.
   - c. Spanish.

6. On the whole, the article tells about
   - a. the way some peoples were named.
   - b. generals who tell jokes about ganders.
   - c. pioneers who went to live in England.

7. Which statement does the article lead you to believe?
   - a. It is often hard to change a name that has been accepted.
   - b. The people of Michigan do not want a president there.
   - c. The greetings of the pioneers became too familiar.

8. Why were the Indians not called by a more correct name?
   - a. They liked the name because Columbus gave it to them.
   - b. They were really people who belonged in India.
   - c. The word *Indian* had been accepted for a long time.

9. Think about the concept for this group of articles. Which statement seems true both for the article and the concept?
   - a. Names today do not always mean what they meant long ago.
   - b. A Hoosier wanted to be president of the United States.
   - c. The ancient Saxons were the first Native Americans.

Tell It to the Marines!

Do you ever wonder how expressions like "keep your shirt on" or "tell it to the marines!" came into our language? Both these phrases have interesting beginnings.

In pioneer days, when men got into a fight, they often took time off to remove their coats and shirts before they wrestled. The men might be angry and excited, but they could not afford to let their clothing get torn. Furthermore, it was easier to move around without a tight collar and long sleeves. Sometimes other men would try to stop a fight before it began. Then they would advise the battlers "keep your shirt on," meaning "don't fight." Today when someone is told to keep his shirt on, he is being warned to stay calm.

"Tell it to the marines" began as a seafaring expression of disbelief and scorn. Early in the nineteenth century, England organized a special army known as the British Royal Marines. These men often had to cross the seas to fight in other parts of the world. They were fine soldiers, but knew very little about life at sea. Sailors enjoyed telling these men fanciful stories. If sailors tried to fool their own shipmates with tall tales, the scornful reply was, "Tell it to the marines!" These sailors knew that only the marines on board might believe such yarns. Today's marines are not so gullible, but we still use this expression to show our disbelief.

In everyday conversation, do you sometimes say "he double-crossed me" or "she's pulling your leg" or "he threw in the sponge"? There are books in the library that will tell you how these expressions arose. The original meanings may surprise you!

FIND THE ANSWERS

1. In pioneer days, when men got into a fight, they often removed their
   - a. coats and shirts.
   - b. socks and shoes.
   - c. hats and gloves.
   - d. combs and brushes.

2. The word in paragraph 4 that means *first* or *earliest* is
   _____ .

3. The words "of disbelief and scorn" in paragraph 3 describe a seafaring
   _____ .

4. While it is not directly stated, the article suggests that
   - a. phrases in our speech come from many places.
   - b. pioneer men did not know how to stay out of fights.
   - c. the marines told the sailors too many stories.

5. England's special army was known as the
   - a. English Marine Army.
   - b. British Royal Marines.
   - c. Royal Pioneer Marines.

6. On the whole, the article tells about
   - a. how some expressions came into our language.
   - b. life at sea in the nineteenth century.
   - c. sailors who worked in the army.

7. Which statement does the article lead you to believe?
   - a. People in the nineteenth century were very scornful.
   - b. The marines threw sponges at the pioneers.
   - c. Interesting phrases become part of our speech.

8. Why did sailors tell the marines fanciful stories?
   - a. They knew that the marines might believe them.
   - b. They wanted the marines to stay calm and happy.
   - c. They didn't think the pioneers would listen.

9. Think about the concept for this group of articles. Which statement seems true both for the article and for the concept?
   - a. You can only cross the sea if you are a marine.
   - b. Pioneers were always wrestling the marines.
   - c. People may say one thing but mean another.

The Lake That Wasn't There

A group of travelers driving across the Sahara Desert were startled to see a cool, inviting lake suddenly appear in the distance. They gazed with delight at the broad sheet of water sparkling in the sunlight. Busily, they made plans to go swimming as soon as they reached the lake. But their driver, an experienced desert guide, informed the passengers regretfully that when they reached the area ahead, they would find only dust, sand, and rocks.

The travelers insisted that they could see something ahead. Those with cameras were even able to take pictures of the lake the driver said wasn't there! Later they learned that what they had seen was a reflection of the sky on the hot, dry land. Their cameras, like their eyes, had seen the image the light rays had created. They had seen a mirage.

Mirages appear when there are layers of air of different density. Next to the desert floor, the air was hot. Above this hot air was another layer of cooler, more dense air. Light rays passing down from the layer of more dense air into the layer of less dense air were bent upward. The bent rays reflected the sky. This bending of light rays is called *refraction*.

On a clear summer day, drivers may see this kind of mirage on a paved highway. Their eyes tell them that a patch of road ahead is wet. A blanket of hot air lies next to the road surface, which has been warmed by the sun. Light rays bend upward as they pass into this layer. What the drivers see is just a reflection of the sky.

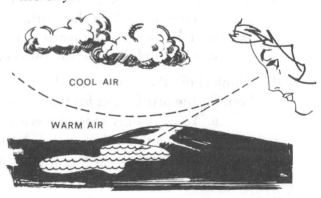

COOL AIR

WARM AIR

FIND THE ANSWERS

1. The travelers took pictures of
   - a. dust on the road.
   - b. rocks in the desert.
   - c. the driver bending rays.
   - d. a reflection of the sky.

2. The word in paragraph 1 that means *surprised* is_____.

3. The words "which has been warmed by the sun" in paragraph 4 describe the road _____.

4. While it is not directly stated, the article suggests that
   - a. desert guides do not let travelers go swimming.
   - b. travelers in the desert take too many pictures.
   - c. mirages can be seen in many different places.

5. The bending of light rays is called
   - a. reflection.
   - b. subtraction.
   - c. refraction.

6. On the whole, the story tells about
   - a. people who drive in the summer.
   - b. mirages, and how they happen.
   - c. travelers who stare at the sky.

7. Which statement does the article lead you to believe?
   - a. Drivers should stay off paved highways in summer.
   - b. Blankets of hot air are better than blankets of wool.
   - c. People see mirages even when they know what causes them.

8. Why could the travelers take pictures of a mirage?
   - a. The camera, like their eyes, could see the image.
   - b. They had new, expensive cameras and good film.
   - c. The driver said they could take the pictures.

9. Think about the concept for this group of articles. Which statement seems true both for the article and for the concept?
   - a. People should never travel in hot, dry places.
   - b. Sometimes people see things that are not there.
   - c. All layers of air have exactly the same density.

The Ship That Was Someplace Else

Gazing out from his hut one day, an explorer in Antarctica was amazed to see a ship. He was right to be startled because his hut was over a hundred miles inland, far from the sea. He knew that even with a telescope he could not possibly see this ship. It would be hidden from him by the curve of the earth. Yet the explorer was not dreaming. A ship did approach Antarctica that day. The man was able to see it because of an unusual trick of light and air called *looming*.

When light passes up from a layer of more dense air to a layer of less dense air, its rays are bent downward. In this case, the more dense layer was close to the ground. Light rays reflected from the ship were bent downward by the atmosphere. It was this bending that enabled the explorer to see the ship, even though it was below the horizon.

Looming may cause distant mountains to appear much closer than they are. It may cause things on the ground to appear elevated in the air. Sometimes objects, like ships at sea, give the appearance of being upside down.

Antarctica is not the only place where looming occurs. It can happen over still, cool bodies of water, usually in winter or early in the morning. Under normal conditions, people in Chicago cannot see across Lake Michigan to the sand dunes on the opposite shore. Yet sometimes looming makes the sand dunes visible. If the air lying low over the lake is much cooler than the air above it, the light rays will bend rather than travel in a straight line.

Looming is usually thought of as one type of mirage.

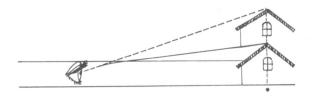

FIND THE ANSWERS

1. One type of mirage is known as
   - a. gloomy.
   - b. bending.
   - c. looming.
   - d. weaving.

2. The word in paragraph 2 that means *thrown back* is _____.

3. The words "like ships at sea" in paragraph 3 describe _____.

4. While it is not directly stated, the article suggests that
   - a. explorers do not belong in Antarctica.
   - b. light rays cannot be reflected any place.
   - c. looming can cause some unusual sights.

5. People in Chicago cannot usually see across Lake Michigan to
   - a. the opposite shore.
   - b. the end of the lake.
   - c. the top of the mountain.

6. On the whole, the article tells about
   - a. a hut that is far from the sea.
   - b. a kind of mirage known as looming.
   - c. cool bodies of water in the winter.

7. Which statement does the article lead you to believe?
   - a. Mirages cannot happen in Antarctica.
   - b. It can be exciting to see a mirage.
   - c. Most explorers come from Chicago.

8. Why was the explorer able to see the ship?
   - a. He saw it because of a bending of light in air.
   - b. He had the most powerful telescope in Antarctica.
   - c. He saw it because the curve of the earth was right.

9. Think about the concept for this group of articles. Which statement seems true both for the article and for the concept?
   - a. Explorers in Antarctica are easily amazed.
   - b. Mountains in Antarctica move around all of the time.
   - c. Our eyes sometimes play tricks on our minds.

The Ground That Gives Way

A person steps on what seems like solid ground but discovers with horror that the ground is giving way underfoot. The person struggles desperately but is trapped. There is no escape. Slowly the person sinks deeper and at last is gone, buried in the treacherous earth. The solid ground was solid only in appearance. It was actually quicksand, which is a deep mass of fine sand mixed with water.

How is quicksand formed? Water pushes up from below the surface and is held by the sand. The grains of sand are forced apart by the water. They cannot hold any weight. The subsurface water may have come from a spring, a river, or a stream. Sometimes pools of water near beaches become filled with sand. When the soil under these pools does not allow for good drainage, the sand can become stretches of quicksand.

Is it true that a person who steps into quicksand is doomed to die? No,

for people have fought their way from quicksand to firm land again. It is panic that creates the condition that can result in death, for the more a person struggles, the worse matters become. Quick movements will make the sand yield temporarily, but then it rushes back and settles solidly around the body.

People trapped in quicksand should either lie back with arms outstretched, or not move at all. When the weight of sand a person's body has displaced equals that person's weight, the victim will stop sinking. With feet held still, and with slow movements of the arms, as in the backstroke in swimming, people have managed to roll to safety and reach firm ground.

FIND THE ANSWERS

1. Quick movements by a person trapped in quicksand will
   - a. help the person reach firm ground.
   - b. make the same sand yield temporarily.
   - c. help prevent panic.
   - d. make the sand hold the person's weight.

2. The word in paragraph 1 that means *dangerous* is _____.

3. The words "as in the backstroke in swimming" in paragraph 4 describe the movements of the _____.

4. While it is not directly stated, the article suggests that
   - a. all ground that looks solid is really quicksand.
   - b. it is a frightening thing to be caught in quicksand.
   - c. only heavy people can be trapped in quicksand.

5. Quicksand is
   - a. a mass of fine sand mixed with water.
   - b. formed only along rivers.
   - c. found below subsurface water.

6. On the whole, the article tells about
   - a. the nature of quicksand.
   - b. stepping into quicksand.
   - c. what solid ground looks like.

7. Which statement does the article lead you to believe?
   - a. People should never try to escape from quicksand.
   - b. Stretches of quicksand are found only under the sea.
   - c. It is hard to keep calm if you fall into quicksand.

8. Why is poor drainage under sand-filled pools dangerous?
   - a. These pools can become filled with water.
   - b. These pools can become stretches of quicksand.
   - c. People who step into them start to fight in panic.

9. Think about the concept for this group of articles. Which statement seems true both for the article and for the concept?
   - a. You cannot always tell solid land by sight.
   - b. People put too many traps in quicksand.
   - c. Water-filled grains of sand hold weight.

The Magic and Drama of Dance

For hundreds of years, audiences have filled the halls and theaters where dancers perform ballets. Some ballets, like *The Sleeping Beauty*, tell a story. Others simply try to create a mood, or represent the music they are being danced to. But at all ballets, dancers use their movements to create a new world for the audience.

One of the greatest dancers of all time was a British woman named Margot Fonteyn, who danced for over 40 years. Because she never stopped dancing, she was able to maintain her strength and grace for a long time. In 1976, when she was 57, Margot Fonteyn danced in a ballet called *The Merry Widow*.

In America, dance was transformed by a dancer and choreographer named Martha Graham. The Asian Americans and blacks of her early company were the first of their races to perform in American modern dance. In the dances that Martha Graham choreographed, characters used movements to show feelings such as fear, anger, and jealousy. For this reason, her dances sometimes shocked audiences. Martha Graham died in 1991, but the dance company that she founded still performs all over the world.

Alvin Ailey was another great choreographer. Many of Alvin Ailey's modern dances used folk music and jazz from the South, where he grew up. Some of his works had political themes. Alvin Ailey's dance called *Survivors,* which was performed in 1986, was based on the anti-apartheid movement in South Africa. Although Ailey died in 1989, the Alvin Ailey Dance Company still performs today.

1. Margot Fonteyn was a
      a. dancer.   c. choreographer.
      b. ballet.   d. musician.

2. The word in paragraph 3 that means *changed* is _____.

3. The words "one of the greatest dancers of all time" in paragraph 2 describe
   _____   _____.

4. While it is not directly stated, the article suggests that
      a. Martha Graham could not dance, but she could choreograph.
      b. Martha Graham studied with Margot Fonteyn.
      c. Martha Graham's dances were not like anyone else's.

5. Alvin Ailey created a dance called
      a. *The Merry Widow.*
      b. *Survivors.*
      c. *Sleeping Beauty.*

6. On the whole, the article tells about
      a. how to become a ballet dancer.
      b. how dance expresses stories and feelings.
      c. why fewer people are going to ballets.

7. Which statement does the article lead you to believe?
      a. Watching people dance on stage is dull.
      b. Ballets use words to tell stories.
      c. Dancing has much in common with acting.

8. Why did Martha Graham's dances shock audiences?
      a. They showed strong feelings.
      b. The dancers wore strange costumes.
      c. The music was loud.

9. Think about the concept for this group of articles. Which statement seems true for both the article and the concept?
      a. Dancers cannot tell stories as well as actors can.
      b. Ballets are the only dances with happy endings.
      c. People on stage create a world of make-believe.

Neighbors in the Sky

Things are not always what they seem! If you study the stars, you know this statement is true. To the early sky watchers, many stars seemed to be close together in groups, or constellations. The Greeks and Romans gave these constellations names which are still commonly used. But today we know that the stars in these constellations are not close together. They simply lie in the same field of vision. We have learned that because two things can be seen at once, they are not necessarily near or next to each other. You might, for example, see two traffic lights at once even though the lights might be several blocks apart.

There are eighty-eight constellations in the sky, about sixty of which can be seen from the Northern Hemisphere. Stargazers cannot see all sixty constellations simultaneously, however. Only about twenty-four are visible at a time.

The Big Dipper, which is part of the constellation known as Ursa Major, or the Great Bear, is easily located in the sky. The first two stars in the handle of the Dipper are Alkaid (al kād') and Mizar (mī'zär). These two stars seem to be neighbors, but Mizar lies 78 light years away and Alkaid is an additional 120 light years farther from our eyes. A light year is the distance light travels in one year.

The large red star in the shoulder of the constellation known as Orion (ə rī'ən), the Giant, is 300 light years away from our planet. The blue star in Orion's knee is 540 light years away.

You can see why, in studying the sky, astronomers quickly became aware that things are not always what they seem.

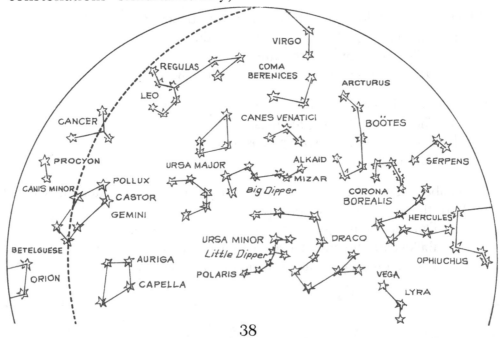

FIND THE ANSWERS

1. About sixty constellations can be seen from
   - a. the Southern Hemisphere.
   - b. the Northern Hemisphere.
   - c. the Big Dipper.
   - d. Orion, the Giant.

2. The word in paragraph 2 that means *at the same time* is

   _____ .

3. The words "in the shoulder of the constellation known as Orion" in paragraph 4 describe the large red _____ .

4. While it is not directly stated, the article suggests that
   - a. there are too many constellations in the sky.
   - b. it is very difficult to locate the Big Dipper.
   - c. ancient people were very interested in the stars.

5. The Big Dipper is part of the constellation called
   - a. Great Alkaid.
   - b. Big Mizar.
   - c. Ursa Major.

6. On the whole, the article tells about
   - a. the position of stars in the constellations.
   - b. Greeks who called Romans names.
   - c. the different colors of the stars.

7. Which statement does the article lead you to believe?
   - a. All ancient Romans were stargazers.
   - b. The sky is full of red and blue stars.
   - c. The stars are a great distance from earth.

8. Why do the stars in constellations seem close?
   - a. They are nearer to each other than to us.
   - b. They lie in the same field of vision.
   - c. They are too easily located in the sky.

9. Think about the concept for this group of articles. Which statement seems true both for the article and for the concept?
   - a. We cannot always trust our vision.
   - b. Two things cannot be seen at once.
   - c. A dipper must have a large handle.

The Shrinking Moon

The full moon climbs over the eastern horizon and hangs like a huge orange globe in the sky. A few hours later, the moon is overhead but seems to have changed. The huge orange globe has become a small silver disk. What has happened? Why has the orange color disappeared? Why does the moon seem so much smaller and farther away now that it is overhead?

The moon appears orange on the horizon because we view it through the dust of the atmosphere. The overhead moon does not really shrink as it moves away from the horizon. Our eyes inform us that the overhead moon is farther away. But in this position the moon is actually closer to our eyes than when it is near the horizon.

The change in size is a trick our eyes and minds play on us. When the moon is low in the sky, we can compare its size with familiar objects. It is easy to see that the moon is much larger than trees or buildings, for example. When the moon is high in the sky, however, it is hard to compare it with objects on earth. Compared to the vastness of the sky, the moon seems small.

There is another reason why the moon seems to shrink. We are used to gazing at objects straight ahead of us. When an object is difficult to see, our eyes have to strain to focus on it. When we tilt our heads back to look up, there is a similar strain. Looking at something from an unaccustomed position can fool you into believing an object is smaller or farther away than it is. However, scientists do not yet understand completely why the moon seems to shrink as it rises in the sky.

FIND THE ANSWERS

1. The line we see between earth and sky is the
   - a. atmosphere.
   - b. weather.
   - c. horizon.
   - d. comparison.

2. The word in paragraph 4 that means *looking* is _____.

3. The words "like a huge orange globe in the sky" in paragraph 1 refer to the

   _____.

4. While it is not directly stated, the article suggests that
   - a. the moon is too close to earth these days.
   - b. we should not gaze straight ahead of us.
   - c. the size of an object can seem to change.

5. When the moon appears orange, we see it through the
   - a. dust of the atmosphere.
   - b. dust in our curtains.
   - c. trees on the ground.

6. On the whole, the article tells about
   - a. seeming changes in the size of the moon.
   - b. the exact color of the moon in the sky.
   - c. the size of trees and buildings on earth.

7. Which statement does the article lead you to believe?
   - a. An orange moon is better than a silver moon.
   - b. We cannot make measurements with our eyes alone.
   - c. It is good to strain your eyes to look at things.

8. Why is it hard to look at objects overhead?
   - a. We cannot tilt our heads back too far.
   - b. Our eyes have to strain to focus on them.
   - c. Objects overhead are always shrinking.

9. Think about the concept for this group of articles. Which statement seems true both for the article and for the concept?
   - a. We do not see the moon as it really is.
   - b. The moon is really a huge orange globe.
   - c. Our moon is beginning to shrink too much.

A Rich Plum for Horner

Do you remember the nursery rhyme about Little Jack Horner who stuck his thumb into a pie and pulled out a plum? Many nursery rhymes were nonsense verses made up to entertain children long ago. The rhymes were repeated to each new generation of children. But some rhymes were not meant for children at all. Many of them ridiculed dishonest people in high places while others were sharp comments on the political happenings of the day. The true meaning of the rhymes was usually hidden under what appeared to be nonsense. Little Jack Horner is one example of this kind of rhyme.

There was a real man named John Horner who lived in England during the reign of King Henry VIII. King Henry decided to break up the large, valuable estates that belonged to the Church and give the land to his friends. Somehow the rich lands of the Abbey of Mells came to Horner, who was a steward in the household of an important church offical. Horner's enemies may have been envious of his sudden wealth. Or the King's enemies may have resented the way the King distributed other people's property. In any case, before long the rhyme about Little Jack Horner began to be heard.

There may even have been an actual pie! In those days, valuable papers were baked inside pies at times to keep them safe from thieves. The deed to the Abbey's lands may have been baked into a pie.

Stories about the manner in which Horner got his land differ, for no one seems to know now exactly how it happened. But what we can say with certainty is that Horner did indeed get his plum!

LITTLE JACK HORNER,
SAT IN THE CORNER,
EATING HIS CHRISTMAS PIE;
HE STUCK IN HIS THUMB,
AND PULLED OUT A PLUM,
AND CRIED, "WHAT A BRIGHT BOY AM I."

1. Horner lived in England during the reign of
   a. King Henry VIII.   c. King Herbert III.
   b. King Harold XX.   d. King Hal II.

2. The word in paragraph 1 that means *made fun of* is

   _____ .

3. The words "who stuck his thumb into a pie" in paragraph 1 describe Little

   _____   _____ .

4. While it is not directly stated, the article suggests that
   a. there are interesting stories behind many rhymes.
   b. nursery rhymes always praised dishonest people.
   c. Jack Horner wrote a nursery rhyme for the King.

5. King Henry decided to break up estates that belonged
   a. to his friends.
   b. to the Church.
   c. to pie makers.

6. On the whole, the article tells about
   a. the real meaning of Little Jack Horner.
   b. paper pies that were baked for the King.
   c. plums that are too rich to go into pies.

7. Which statement does the article lead you to believe?
   a. King Henry VIII was a good friend to the Church.
   b. King Henry VIII did not have any enemies at all.
   c. King Henry VIII was a powerful and ruthless king.

8. Why were some nursery rhymes written?
   a. They were meant to teach nonsense to Jack Horner.
   b. They were meant to comment on political happenings.
   c. The King liked to hear children repeat nonsense.

9. Think about the concept for this group of articles. Which statement seems true both for the article and for the concept?
   a. Stories may mean more than we think.
   b. The Abbey of Mells was happy to lose his land.
   c. King Henry VIII was not a real king.

What Goes with the Crown?

Elizabeth II was crowned Queen of Great Britain and the British Commonwealth in 1953. She rode to her coronation in a gold, horse-drawn coach made for King George III. On her head was a jeweled crown made for King Charles II. The coronation chair in which she sat had been made for King Edward I more than 650 years ago. Under the chair was the Stone of Scone. On this historic rock early Scottish rulers had been crowned.

Great Britain has kept the monarchy and many of the ancient traditions that surround the crown. But Queen Elizabeth II is a constitutional monarch with little real power over her people.

In the Middle Ages, the monarch was above the law. Subjects who displeased the ruler were likely to lose their lands, their money, or their lives. The ruler could call up armies and fight wars at any time.

The power of England's monarch was first limited by the Magna Carta, signed by King John in 1215. This charter gave some rights to the barons and to the middle-class people. It set a pattern by which the monarch ruled under law.

In 1649 King Charles I was executed, and for a time England had no ruler at all. When the monarchy was restored, there was a balance of power between the ruler and the legislative body, Parliament.

Laws passed later took more and more powers away from the monarch. The powers were given to Parliament and to elected officials. By gradual stages, the monarch ceased to be the ruler of the country. The monarchy became a symbol rather than a true center of power. Today the person who wears the British crown reigns without ruling.

1. The coronation chair was made 650 years ago for
    a. Queen Elizabeth.
    c. Queen Mary.
    b. King Edward I.
    d. King George.

2. The word in paragraph 5 that means *brought back* is _____.

3. The words "that surround the crown" in paragraph 2 describe the ancient

   _____ .

4. While it is not directly stated, the article suggests that
    a. Queen Elizabeth is a powerful ruler.
    b. no one gives the Queen anything new.
    c. England likes some of the old traditions.

5. The power of England's rulers was limited by
    a. middle age.
    b. the Magna Carta.
    c. middle-class people.

6. On the whole, the article tells about
    a. the rulers in England.
    b. a gold, horse-drawn coach.
    c. the Stone of Scone.

7. Which statement does the article lead you to believe?
    a. Queen Elizabeth signed the Magna Carta.
    b. Parliament gave King John the Stone of Scone.
    c. People long ago had much to fear from rulers.

8. Why is the English monarchy only a symbol?
    a. The rulers refuse to wear their crowns.
    b. The ruler is not the true center of power.
    c. The early Scottish kings kept the monarchy.

9. Think about the concept for this group of articles. Which statement seems true both for the article and for the concept?
    a. Chairs in England have stones under them.
    b. The barons signed a paper for King John.
    c. A coronation does not make a ruler powerful.

The Giant Optical Illusion

The Parthenon is an ancient Greek temple built in Athens about 438 B.C. Many people think that the Parthenon is one of the world's most beautiful buildings. It has a grace and a balance that have pleased the eyes of people for centuries.

Architects who have studied the Parthenon know that the Parthenon is a giant optical illusion. An optical illusion is a trick our eyes play on us. All the seemingly straight lines of the Parthenon are actually curves. These curves did not happen by accident. The ancient Greeks, who were fine engineers as well as excellent artists, knew that straight lines can sometimes appear to be curved! So they designed their columns to *look* straight.

Try drawing two long parallel lines on paper. Do they seem to look closer together in the middle than at the ends? A tall column is likely to look pinched halfway up along its height,

too. The columns of the Parthenon look as if they stand perfectly straight. Actually, they are slightly swollen in the middle and slant inward a little at the top. If lines were drawn up along opposite sides of the columns, these lines would meet about one mile above the building.

A platform of three steps forms the base on which the Parthenon rests. These steps have strong horizontal lines that balance the vertical lines of the columns. But the steps are not really level and flat! They curve up in the middle because if they were absolutely straight, they would appear to curve down. The line of the top step, if continued at both ends, would form a circle with a radius of 3½ miles.

When is a curved line not a curved line? When our eyes tell us it is straight!

46

1. The Parthenon is
   a. in the London Museum.　　c. an ancient Greek temple.
   b. a skyscraper in Paris.　　d. a building in Rome.

2. The word in paragraph 2 that means *drew up the plans for* is

   _____ .

3. The words "that balance the vertical lines of the columns" in paragraph 4

   describe the horizontal _____ .

4. While it is not directly stated, the article suggests that
   a. the ancient Greeks couldn't draw a straight line.
   b. most architects don't think much of the Parthenon.
   c. we still admire the work of ancient Greeks.

5. The base on which the Parthenon rests is made up of
   a. three steps.
   b. five circles.
   c. 3½ miles.

6. On the whole, the article tells about
   a. the design of the Parthenon.
   b. lines meeting at the end of a mile.
   c the horizontal lines of steps.

7. Which statement does the article lead you to believe?
   a. The Greeks were only allowed to build one temple.
   b. The Greeks knew a great deal about optical illusions.
   c. You cannot draw horizontal lines without vertical lines.

8. What makes the steps look level and flat?
   a. They curve up in the middle.
   b. They are level and flat.
   c. They curve down in the middle.

9. Think about the concept for this group of articles. Which statement seems true
   both for the article and for the concept?
   a. The ancient Greeks built strange buildings by accident.
   b. It is hard to draw two parallel lines.
   c. Some lines that we see as straight are really curved.

Not What They Seem

What do we see when we go to the movies? Do we see real movement or only the illusion of movement? What is a "motion" picture?

A motion picture is actually a series of still pictures shown one after another so quickly that the human eye blends them together. In one second, twenty-four separate pictures are flashed on the screen. Between one picture and the next there is an instant of darkness while the projector moves the film forward. Human eyes are not quick enough to see these pictures separately. Our eyes hold one image until the next is shown. We are not aware of the instant when the screen is dark.

Are still pictures that seem to move the only illusion in movies? No. Motion pictures present us with many illusions. Suppose there is a scene showing a storm at sea. Often the ships used in these scenes are models, only inches long, and the waves only ripples. Such scenes are frequently staged in tanks the size of small swimming pools. Special machines produce waves to order inside the tanks.

In huge air-conditioned studios, moviemakers can produce any kind of weather for the camera. Rain comes from overhead sprinklers, wind from giant fans. Smoke or fog is likely to be vapor rising from blocks of dry ice concealed behind the scenery.

A rider gallops into the street of a dusty Western town. Is it a real town? Sometimes. But often the street is lined with false fronts. Rooms in buildings may be just stage sets with one or two walls and no ceilings to make it easy for cameras to film the action.

In movies, many things are not what they seem!

FIND THE ANSWERS

1. A motion picture is made up of a series of
   - a. dark films.
   - b. human eyes.
   - c. fast flashes.
   - d. still pictures.

2. The word in paragraph 4 that means *hidden* is _____.

3. The words "only inches long" in paragraph 3 describe ships used as

   _____ .

4. While it is not directly stated, the article suggests that
   - a. the movies make use of many special machines.
   - b. people do not ride real horses in the Westerns.
   - c. all our rain comes from overhead sprinklers.

5. Rooms in buildings may be just
   - a. tiny models.
   - b. dusty towns.
   - c. stage sets.

6. On the whole, the article tells about
   - a. projectors that move films.
   - b. illusions in motion pictures.
   - c. waves that make ripples in pools.

7. Which statement does the article lead you to believe?
   - a. We can always see the projector moving the film.
   - b. Special machines produce the waves in the ocean.
   - c. We enjoy the illusions created in the movies.

8. Why can't we see the separate pictures on the screen?
   - a. The air conditioning is too strong.
   - b. Smoke and fog get into our eyes.
   - c. Human eyes are not quick enough.

9. Think about the concept for this group of articles. Which statement seems true both for the article and for the concept?
   - a. Movies can only be made outside on nice days.
   - b. We cannot always tell the difference between illusion and reality.
   - c. All smoke and fog comes from blocks of dry ice.

It All Began with Billiard Balls

John W. Hyatt, a printer in Albany, New York, developed Celluloid in 1869 as a new material for making billiard balls!

Until the 1860s, billiard balls were made of ivory. Ivory was scarce and costly. Because of this, an English manufacturer offered a prize of $10,-000 to any inventor who could make a substitute material. Celluloid was the result. Hyatt made it by combining camphor with acid-treated cotton fibers under pressure.

Manufacturers soon found other uses for this valuable new material beside billiard balls. Combs, toothbrush handles, cases for clocks, and eyeglass frames were made. They were just a few of the Celluloid products that began to be sold to the public.

Manufacturers learned to make thin, flat sheets of Celluloid. This made it possible for them to produce such things as stiff white collars for shirts and curtains for carriages and buggies.

In 1889, George Eastman used Celluloid to make the first roll of photographic film. The whole motion picture industry is based on this development.

Celluloid was only the first of many new artificial materals we call *plastics*. A number of these products have been found useful in ways that were not at all what the inventors had in mind.

Cellophane, the first of the transparent wrapping materials, was produced by a Swiss inventor who was seeking a stainproof tablecloth. Bakelite, widely used for electrical parts, telephone mouthpieces, and the handles of cooking pots, was produced by a New York chemist seeking a new kind of varnish.

In today's world, plastics are used in many different ways in such widely separated fields as medicine, architecture, and space programs. And it all began with billiard balls!

FIND THE ANSWERS

1. Manufacturers learned to make Celluloid in
    a. thin, flat sheets.　　　c. varnish.
    b. thick eyeglasses.　　　d. Switzerland.

2. The word in paragraph 2 that means *putting together* is

    _____ .

3. The words "who was seeking a stainproof tablecloth" in paragraph 7 describe

    a Swiss _____ .

4. While it is not directly stated, the article suggests that
    a. printers have to play billiards.
    b. some things happen by chance.
    c. Celluloid products are not good.

5. The first of the transparent wrapping materials was
    a. movie film.
    b. Bakelite.
    c. cellophane.

6. On the whole, the article tells about
    a. the invention of plastic materials.
    b. a printer who lived in Albany, New York.
    c. a big prize for making real ivory.

7. Which statement does the article lead you to believe?
    a. Plastics can only be used in one field.
    b. Swiss inventors are slower than English inventors.
    c. People were very inventive in using plastics.

8. Why did the English manufacturer offer a prize?
    a. He wanted to find a substitute for ivory.
    b. Billiard balls were thin and flat.
    c. He wanted to create a stainproof tablecloth.

9. Think about the concept for this group of articles. Which statement seems true both for the article and for the concept?
    a. Billiard balls make very good toothbrush handles.
    b. One product may sometimes be substituted for another.
    c. Celluloid is not one of the artificial materials.

Bending Towers and Swaying Skyscrapers

Steel seems very stiff and rigid, but actually it is elastic. Cast iron is brittle and will break under stress. Steel can bend and stretch a little. This wonderful quality of steel makes possible today's skyscrapers and the tall towers that support suspension bridges.

Tall buildings have to withstand the force of winds pressing against their broad, flat surfaces. A hurricane wind blowing 100 miles an hour exerts a tremendous force on the vertical surface facing the wind. All this giant push is on just one side of the building. If the building were perfectly rigid, it might break apart.

Modern skyscrapers are built around a framework of steel beams welded together. The steel bends a little, the top of the building sways as much as six inches, and there is no damage.

The towers of suspension bridges are up to 750 feet tall. They not only support the cables that carry the weight of the long roadway but also the weight of cars and trucks using the bridge.

What happens when there is heavy traffic on one end of the bridge and none on the other end? The load the towers support is unbalanced and the pull on them is uneven. But nothing breaks. The towers bend a little, leaning toward the heavily loaded end of the bridge to ease the strain. The tops of the towers can shift as much as three feet in either direction because they are built of steel.

A bridge tower that can bend a little is stronger than one that is rigid. And a skyscraper that sways a little is safer than one that stands still.

FIND THE ANSWERS

1. Tops of bridge towers can shift as much as
    - a. seven yards.
    - b. three feet.
    - c. ten inches.
    - d. one foot.

2. The word in paragraph 2 that means *puts forth* is _____.

3. The words "that sways a little" in paragraph 6 refer to a

    _____ .

4. While it is not directly stated, the article suggests that
    - a. towers that bend are not safe.
    - b. skyscrapers should not sway.
    - c. bridges should not be rigid.

5. Tall buildings have to withstand the force
    - a. of steel.
    - b. of giants.
    - c. of winds.

6. On the whole, the article tells about
    - a. the importance of steel in building.
    - b. heavy traffic across small bridges.
    - c. towers that keep shifting around.

7. Which statement does the article lead you to believe?
    - a. Cast iron is used as a framework for skyscrapers.
    - b. Steel beams welded together damage buildings.
    - c. We could not get along very well without steel.

8. Why will cast iron break under stress?
    - a. It is brittle.
    - b. It is fragile.
    - c. It is heavy.

9. Think about the concept for this group of articles. Which statement seems true both for the article and for the concept?
    - a. Bridges with tall towers are one-sided.
    - b. Some things that appear stationary do move.
    - c. Steel is a very stiff, rigid material.

In the Land of the Ice Giants

Thor (thôr), the Norse god of thunder and lightning, was very angry with the Ice Giants, for they killed the plant life on earth with their fearful blasts of freezing wind. Thor, who wanted the earth to stay green and fruitful, finally resolved to punish the Ice Giants. Therefore, taking the fire spirit Loki along, Thor set out for the kingdom of the Ice Giants, determined to reach it that same day. But when night came, Thor and Loki still had quite a distance to travel.

"What a bleak country this is," Loki complained. "I can see no shelter. Even if there were shelter somewhere, we could not find it in this miserable fog."

"I see the outline of a most peculiar house," Thor replied, squinting into the fog. "It will have to do for a night's lodging."

When Thor and Loki reached the shelter, they had to fumble their way into the odd-looking structure, for there was no light to guide them. The weary Thor had just dozed off when he was rudely awakened by Loki.

"An earthquake!" Loki bellowed in Thor's ear. Loki was right. The ground was trembling violently beneath them. Loki rushed from the shelter with Thor close behind. Outside, the exhausted Thor threw himself to the ground and was soon asleep again. Loki also fell into deep slumber. Next morning, when they awoke, they were amazed to see that they had had a companion. Close beside them, a giant lay snoring. He snored so hard that the ground quivered beneath them.

"There is our earthquake!" Loki said, bursting into laughter.

At the sound of Loki's voice, the giant awoke, yawned, peered about, and picked up the odd shelter Thor and Loki had entered during the foggy night. Now Thor and Loki could plainly see that it was the giant's glove. They had spent part of the night in the thumb!

The giant seemed friendly enough, and even offered to guide the travelers to the land they were seeking. But when night fell again, they were still not at their destination. Sleepily, the giant offered Loki and Thor food from a pack he carried, but fell asleep before Thor could open it. Angry because he was tired and hungry, and because the giant's snores were shaking the land again, Thor took his hammer and gave the giant three terrible blows.

The giant brushed his forehead and muttered drowsily, "How these falling leaves tickle one."

Next morning, the giant showed Thor and Loki a shortcut to the ice castle belonging to Utgard (üt' gärd), King of the Ice Giants.

"What tiny creatures you are," said Utgard, when Thor and Loki were brought to him. "Can my eyes have deceived me? Are you the mighty Thor and the great Loki about whom we have heard so much? What can such puny ones do?"

Loki, who had not eaten for three days, said, "Bring me food. I wager I will outeat anyone here."

Immediately the king commanded that a great wooden trough be filled with meat and placed before Loki.

"My cook shall start at one end and you at the other," Utgard said. "Let us see who can eat more."

Loki fell to with a will, and ate his way clear to the middle of the trough. But when he looked up, he discovered that the cook had eaten the meat, the bones, and his share of the wooden trough as well!

"I thought you were hungry," said Utgard, sneering.

"I am thirsty," Thor growled. "Bring me the biggest vessel in the castle, and I shall outdrink anyone here."

The king had a large horn brought in at once. "If you are really thirsty," he said, "you can empty this horn with a single swallow." Thor raised the horn to his lips and began to drink.

He drank so much that he thought he would burst. But the liquid in the horn remained level with the rim.

"You can't have been thirsty after all," Utgard said, with contempt. "I hear you are strong. Perhaps you can attempt to lift my cat."

"Certainly," Thor replied, but no matter how he heaved and tugged, he could barely raise even one of the cat's paws from the ground.

"What? You cannot lift my cat?" Utgard hooted triumphantly. "Then you must wrestle my old nurse. Even a weakling should be able to do that."

But Thor found this task impossible too.

"It seems," Thor admitted angrily, "that we are not so powerful as we believed ourselves to be."

Next morning, Utgard took Thor and Loki to the boundary of the Ice Giant's kingdom. "Before you go," he said, "I must warn you. Never return or we shall have to destroy you. You are too dangerous for our liking."

"What?" Thor cried in surprise. "You fear two such weaklings as we?"

"Weaklings?" Utgard replied. "We were forced to use our strongest magic against you. Had the giant you struck with your hammer not put an invisible mountain between you and him, you would have killed him! And you, Loki," Utgard continued. "The cook who ate more than you was the Giant Logi, god of wild fire."

"And my drinking horn?" Thor asked slowly.

"It was attached to the ocean," Utgard replied. "You almost drank the ocean dry! The cat, whose paw you barely lifted, was the terrible giant snake that circles the world. And the nurse was Old Age. No one can fight Old Age, not even the gods."

"You tricked us," Thor cried, raising his hammer in anger. But even as Thor spoke, Utgard disappeared, and all the land was swallowed in swirling mists. The disappointed Thor and Loki returned home. But they had taught the Ice Giants a lesson, for these giants now sent icy winds to earth only in those months men later named winter.

971 words

II

People's Ideas About Things Change from Time to Time

In this section, you will read about changes that occur in our ways of thinking about things. You will read about this in the areas of history, biology, economics, anthropology, geography, Earth science, space, political science, art, and engineering.

Keep these questions in mind when you are reading.

1. What are some big ideas that are no longer the same?

2. What caused the ideas to change?

3. Do we benefit from changing our ideas?

4. Can you think of ideas that you have now that are different from what they used to be?

5. Do changes of ideas cause problems?

Look on pages 7-8 for help with words you don't understand in this section.

It All Began with Some Convicts

On May 13, 1787, a fleet of English ships set sail for Australia with about 750 people. These men and women were no ordinary passengers. They were convicts being sent to Australia as punishment for their crimes.

Laws in England during this period were very harsh, and people were punished severely for even the smallest crimes. Someone could be sentenced to death for hunting on another person's property or be put to death for chopping down someone else's tree. For many other crimes, the punishment was "transportation." Guilty men and women were shipped to a distant land where they were forced to work without pay. Often children were shipped to other lands, too.

In 1770, Captain Cook had discovered the continent of Australia and claimed it for England. At first, England found no use for this vast land on the other side of the world, but then the American Revolution took place. England could no longer ship its convicts to the American colonies. So it turned to Australia as a good place for its prisoners.

A former naval captain was picked to accompany the convicts to the new colony. His job was to help them build a settlement that he would govern. The captain was glad to go. He believed the convicts could learn to live in peace. He felt they would obey the laws in a new country.

In January 1788, the English fleet and its strange cargo landed in Australia. After days of searching, the captain found a fine harbor. The land nearby had trees and streams. The convict colony made a new beginning here. Australia's history had begun.

FIND THE ANSWERS

1. Laws in England during the 1700s were very
    a. kind.   c. harsh.
    b. easy.   d. light.

2. The word in paragraph 4 that means *go along with* is _____ .

3. The words "which he would govern" in paragraph 4 refer to the

   _____ .

4. While it is not directly stated, the article suggests that
    a. people were not often punished in England long ago.
    b. England's laws have changed very much since 1787.
    c. Captain Cook claimed Australia for the convicts.

5. For many crimes, the punishment was
    a. "transportation."
    b. "communication."
    c. "education."

6. On the whole, the article tells about
    a. a fleet of English ships.
    b. hunting on other people's property.
    c. a convict settlement in Australia.

7. Which statement does the article lead you to believe?
    a. All English fleets have very strange cargoes.
    b. A new chance may be good for many people.
    c. The people on the English ships were ordinary.

8. Why did England send convicts to Australia?
    a. It wanted to make Captain Cook happy about Australia.
    b. It could no longer send convicts to America.
    c. It wanted convicts to find a fine harbor and good land.

9. Think about the concept for this group of articles. Which statement seems true both for the article and for the concept?
    a. Former naval captains always start new colonies.
    b. The American Revolution took place in Australia.
    c. A great country may grow from a small colony.

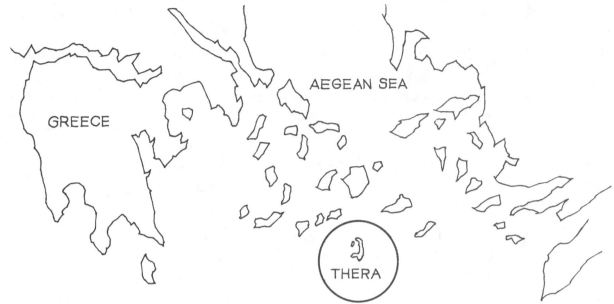

GREECE

AEGEAN SEA

THERA

The Search for a "Lost Continent"

Around 355 B.C. in ancient Greece, the great teacher Plato told a story about a place called Atlantis. Plato described Atlantis as a continent in the Atlantic Ocean. He said it had been the home of a powerful people who were destroyed when the continent was suddenly swallowed by the sea.

Ever since Plato's time, people have wondered if the story about Atlantis was really true. Was there ever such a place as Atlantis? During the Middle Ages, many people believed in the legend of Atlantis. Some men even made voyages to find the "lost continent." Later, most people believed Atlantis to be just a myth. Scientists could find no evidence to show that such a place had ever existed.

Ideas change in time, however, for now some scientists think that Atlantis may have been a real place.

A Greek professor has offered a new theory. He says that Atlantis was not a continent in the Atlantic Ocean but an island called Thera in the Aegean Sea. The professor says that 3,500 years ago much of Thera collapsed into the sea when a volcano erupted. He thinks that before the explosion Thera had been the home of a people called Minoans (mə nō′ ənz). The Minoans were sea traders who ruled the Aegean Sea from 2000 B.C. to 1250 B.C.

Scientists who have come to investigate Thera have found an ancient city buried beneath volcanic ash and stone. It appears that the people who lived in the city had an advanced civilization. They were probably Minoans.

Is Thera the "lost continent" of Atlantis? No one may ever know for certain. Atlantis may remain a riddle without an answer.

1. Plato said that Atlantis was in the
   - a. Arctic Sea.
   - c. Indian Ocean.
   - b. Red Sea.
   - d. Atlantic Ocean.

2. The word in paragraph 3 that means *fell down* is _____.

3. The words "who ruled the Aegean Sea" in paragraph 3 describe the sea

   _____ known as Minoans.

4. While it is not directly stated, the article suggests that
   - a. there was no such teacher as Plato.
   - b. the ancient Greeks destroyed Atlantis.
   - c. people want to know more about Atlantis.

5. The ancient Minoans were
   - a. scientists.
   - b. sea traders.
   - c. too advanced.

6. On the whole, the article tells about
   - a. Greece around the year 355 B.C.
   - b. cities under volcanic ash.
   - c. a land that may have existed.

7. Which statement does the article lead you to believe?
   - a. All legends and myths are absolutely true.
   - b. Atlantis is a good place for Greek professors.
   - c. It is still possible that the riddle may be solved.

8. Why did Thera collapse into the sea?
   - a. A volcano erupted.
   - b. Stones buried it.
   - c. No one believed in it.

9. Think about the concept for this group of articles. Which statement seems true both for the article and for the concept?
   - a. There are different theories about Atlantis.
   - b. Everyone knows where the lost continent is.
   - c. Plato was a Greek teacher who lived in Atlantis.

Apple of Gold

Long ago, the love apple decorated flower gardens as an ornamental plant. The plant's small yellow flowers were not very showy, but it bore beautiful fruit, round, smooth, and shiny, which turned bright red or yellow as it ripened. It was beautiful but poisonous, or so most people believed. Other people believed it had magic powers to cause love.

Early Spanish explorers who found this plant growing wild in South and Central America carried it back to Europe. These plants appeared in gardens in Italy as early as 1554. They must have been the kind that bears yellow fruit, because the Italians called the plant *pomi d'oro* (pō′ mē dō′ rō), or apple of gold. By 1750, the plant was grown as a curious ornamental plant throughout Europe. Some people were even daring enough to eat the fruit.

In 1781 in America, Thomas Jefferson raised and ate love apples, but few followed his example. Thirty years later, the love apples were used as food in Louisiana, and by 1835, a few people in the northern states were willing to experiment with them, too. But even as late as 1900, there were people who still believed that these "apples of gold" were poisonous.

Although people did not eat the fruit of this plant, they liked looking at it in their gardens. Later, when they learned it was both good-tasting and good for them, they moved the love apple plant from the flower garden to the vegetable garden. They learned to call it by a new name — tomato.

The apple of gold has lost its place in the flower garden. But today the tomato, grown in hundreds of varieties, is one of the three most popular vegetables in the United States.

FIND THE ANSWERS

1. One of the three most popular vegetables in the United States is
   - a. the cucumber.
   - b. the squash.
   - c. the tomato.
   - d. the onion.

2. The word in paragraph 3 that means *try out* or *test* is

   _____ .

3. The words "which turned bright red or yellow as it ripened" in paragraph 1

   describe the beautiful _____ .

4. While it is not directly stated, the article suggests that
   - a. some people are afraid to try new things.
   - b. all poisonous fruits are really tomatoes.
   - c. Northerners are more daring than Southerners.

5. The tomato plant was carried back to Europe by
   - a. Central Americans.
   - b. Spanish explorers.
   - c. Thomas Jefferson.

6. On the whole, the article tells about
   - a. poisonous fruits in America.
   - b. Italians who are very curious.
   - c. the history of the tomato plant.

7. Which statement does the article lead you to believe?
   - a. Early Spanish explorers found wild plants in Italy.
   - b. People who eat fruit are very daring.
   - c. Tomatoes are one of our most important crops.

8. Why did people raise this plant in their gardens?
   - a. They liked looking at it.
   - b. They thought gold would grow.
   - c. It was the only plant they had.

9. Think about the concept for this group of articles. Which statement seems true both for the article and for the concept?
   - a. The apple of gold belongs only in flower gardens.
   - b. What is not popular today may be popular tomorrow.
   - c. Thomas Jefferson ate all his ornamental plants.

The Mysterious "Little Animals"

Do worms form from cheese and wood? Do insects hatch from mud? Long ago people believed new life could form this way. We call this theory that life can spring from non-living things *spontaneous generation.*

Long before the 1800s, scientists knew about the microscopic forms of life we call *bacteria.* But in those early days, scientists called these tiny living things *animalcules,* or little animals. A few scientists thought that little animals caused some diseases. But they believed that these mysterious little animals came from nonliving material. So their knowledge about bacteria did not help them as long as they continued to believe in spontaneous generation.

Later, scientists realized that worms and insects hatched from eggs laid by living creatures. But they still did not know where bacteria came from.

In the 1800s, a chemist named Louis Pasteur was working in Paris to help winemakers. They complained of the bitter taste of their wine. Pasteur's experiments showed that bacteria spoiled the wine. The winemakers thought the bacteria sprang to life from the wine. Pasteur proved that the bacteria were already in the wine or in the air. He had the wine heated and then sealed from the air. Wine that was sterilized this way did not spoil.

Pasteur had discovered how to preserve foods and make them safe to eat. But he did much more than that. He disproved the theory of spontaneous generation. He proved that bacteria come from other bacteria, just as all complex forms of life come from forms of life like themselves. He also proved that although bacteria are almost everywhere, they can be controlled. Once people accepted this idea, they were able to control the spread of many diseases.

FIND THE ANSWERS

1. Scientists finally realized that worms and insects
   - a. formed in preserves.
   - b. hatched from eggs.
   - c. sterilized wine.
   - d. made cheese and wood.

2. The word in paragraph 5 that means *proved false* is _____ .

3. The words "these tiny living things" in paragraph 2 describe little animals

   called _____ .

4. While it is not directly stated, the article suggests that
   - a. bitter wine is always very good.
   - b. winemakers complain too much.
   - c. winemakers owed much to Pasteur.

5. The theory that life could spring from nonliving things was called
   - a. spontaneous generation.
   - b. the animal generation.
   - c. the time of animalcules.

6. On the whole, the article tells about
   - a. bacteria found in bitter wine.
   - b. the forms of life called bacteria.
   - c. nonliving things called animals.

7. Which statement does the article lead you to believe?
   - a. Ideas in science can change.
   - b. Scientists are all chemists.
   - c. All scientists live in Paris.

8. Why did it help to heat wine and seal it from air?
   - a. It helped the scientists preserve their food.
   - b. It kept the winemakers very busy.
   - c. Wine sterilized this way did not spoil.

9. Think about the concept for this group of articles. Which statement seems true both for the article and for the concept?
   - a. Future scientists may disprove some of our ideas.
   - b. Scientists were very fond of insects long ago.
   - c. Pasteur wanted a spontaneous generation in Paris.

Tea or Coffee?

The Boston Tea Party did more than just help start a war. It helped change the habits and tastes of the North American people. It turned tea drinkers into coffee drinkers.

Coffee and tea are both products of plants that grow in the tropics. When these beverages were introduced in Europe during the 1600s, they became very profitable businesses.

Coffee reached England before tea did, but once the English tasted tea, it became a favorite mealtime drink. English people were soon buying about two pounds of tea leaves per person per year.

English people who went to North America as colonists took along their taste for tea. They preferred it to coffee until about 1773. In that year, the British Parliament passed the Tea Act, a law that helped to push the colonists into war against the mother country. Among colonists, tea became a symbol of unfair taxation and of England's attempts to control all trading with the colonies. The resentment of the colonists was so strong that once several groups of them boarded English ships in Boston harbor and threw bales of tea into the ocean. After this "Boston Tea Party," drinking tea was called unpatriotic by the colonists. They turned to coffee as their beverage.

Today tea is still the favorite drink in England. On the other side of the Atlantic, things are different. The people of the United States drink about three times as many cups of coffee as cups of tea.

FIND THE ANSWERS

1. Coffee and tea plants grow in
    - a. Great Britain.
    - b. the tropics.
    - c. Boston.
    - d. Parliament.

2. The word in paragraph 4 that means *liked more* is _____.

3. The words "that grow in the tropics" in paragraph 2 tell about the

    _____.

4. While it is not directly stated, the article suggests that
    - a. tea drinkers might go to war.
    - b. the tastes of a people can change.
    - c. the colonists were very strong.

5. Tea became a symbol of
    - a. a good, hot drink.
    - b. unfair taxation.
    - c. parties in Boston.

6. On the whole, the article tells about
    - a. beverages in Europe in the 1600s.
    - b. England's resentment of taxes.
    - c. one reason why Americans drink coffee.

7. Which statement does the article lead you to believe?
    - a. The Boston Tea Party took place in Parliament.
    - b. People should not import berries and leaves.
    - c. The colonists resented England's power over them.

8. Why was the Tea Act not a good idea?
    - a. It helped to push the colonists into war.
    - b. It made coffee become too popular.
    - c. It made English people visit the tropics.

9. Think about the concept for this group of articles. Which statement seems true for both the article and the concept?
    - a. People in England should start drinking coffee.
    - b. People's habits do not always stay the same.
    - c. The Tea Act was an English play in North America.

The City That Came Back to Life

In the early 1900s, a modern city called Manaus (mə naús′) grew up on the Amazon River in the heart of Brazil's tropical rain forest. The residents of Manaus made their living from only one product— rubber.

In the jungle surrounding Manaus, thousands of rubber trees grew wild. Indian workers cut the bark of the rubber trees and collected a milky liquid called *latex*. They hardened the latex into giant balls of rubber. Then oceangoing ships sailed down the Amazon River carrying cargoes of rubber to Europe and the United States. There, factories used the rubber to make such items as raincoats, rubber boots, and automobile tires.

Thousands of people came to Manaus because of the great demand for rubber. Indians came from other parts of Brazil to help gather it, and merchants came to buy and sell it. Manaus became a rich city almost overnight. Wealthy rubber merchants built mansions and a magnificent million-dollar opera house.

Unhappily for Manaus, the rubber boom did not last. An Englishman smuggled rubber-tree seeds out of Brazil. These seeds were used to start rubber plantations in the Far East. The plantation-grown rubber sold for less money than the rubber from Brazil. The price of rubber dropped. Many of the rubber

merchants of Manaus lost their wealth. The once thriving and busy city seemed to go to sleep.

Today, Manaus has come back to life. From the nearby jungle flows an endless stream of products. These products include nuts, plants used in making medicines, and valuable woods such as mahogany and ebony. The people of Manaus have learned that a city cannot afford to depend on only one product.

FIND THE ANSWERS

1. The city of Manaus is in the heart of Brazil's
   - a. tropical rain forest.
   - b. mountain country.
   - c. tropical valleys.
   - d. downtown areas.

2. The word in paragraph 2 that means *around* or *circling* is

   _____ .

3. The words "in the heart of Brazil's tropical rain forest" in paragraph 1 describe

   a modern city called _____ .

4. While it is not directly stated, the article suggests that
   - a. all cities become rich overnight.
   - b. rubber is an important product.
   - c. opera houses belong in rain forests.

5. Seeds were used to start rubber plantations
   - a. in the Far East.
   - b. in South America.
   - c. west of Brazil.

6. On the whole, the article tells about
   - a. an Englishman who smuggled seeds.
   - b. a city built around one product.
   - c. plants used in making medicines.

7. Which statement does the article lead you to believe?
   - a. The people of Manaus now work at many different jobs.
   - b. The price of rubber always stays exactly the same.
   - c. Brazil has too many raincoats and rubber boots.

8. Why has Manaus come back to life?
   - a. The rubber merchants sail on the Amazon.
   - b. Its people get many products from the jungle.
   - c. The city people drink a milky liquid called latex.

9. Think about the concept for this group of articles. Which statement seems true
   both for the article and for the concept?
   - a. There are no valuable woods in Manaus, Brazil.
   - b. Rubber trees look better in the Far East.
   - c. People learn new ways to make a living.

When Women Were "Ladies"

As late as 1800, women's only place was in the home. The idea of women in the business world was unthinkable. No "nice" woman would dream of entering what was strictly a "man's world." Even if she could, what would she do? Men were positive that no woman could handle a job outside her home. This was such a widely accepted idea that when the famous Brontë sisters began writing books in 1846, they disguised themselves by signing their books with men's names.

Teaching was the first profession open to women soon after 1800. But even that was not an easy profession for women to enter because most high schools and colleges were open only to men. Oberlin College in Ohio was the first college in America to accept women.

Hospital nursing became respectable work for women only after Florence Nightingale became famous. Because she was a wealthy and cultured woman, as well as a nurse, people began to believe it was possible for women to nurse the sick and still be "ladies." Miss Nightingale opened England's first training school for nurses in 1860.

The invention of the typewriter in 1867 helped to bring women out of the home and into the business world. Because women had slender, quick fingers, they learned to operate typewriters quickly and well. Businessmen found that they had to hire women for this new kind of work.

By 1900, thousands of women were working at real jobs in schools, hospitals, and offices in both England and America. Some women even managed to become doctors or lawyers. The idea that "nice" women could work in the business world had been accepted.

70

FIND THE ANSWERS

1. Florence Nightingale became famous as a
   - a. teacher.
   - b. rich woman.
   - c. nurse.
   - d. typist.

2. The word in paragraph 1 that means *hid behind something* is
   _____ .

3. The words "the first college in America" in paragraph 2 refer to
   _____ _____ .

4. While it is not directly stated, the article suggests that
   - a. all nurses are wealthy, cultured women.
   - b. nursing is a good profession for women.
   - c. women cannot learn to use typewriters.

5. The first profession open to women after 1800 was
   - a. writing.
   - b. teaching.
   - c. operating.

6. On the whole, the article tells about
   - a. high schools and colleges.
   - b. the famous Brontë sisters.
   - c. women in the business world.

7. Which statement does the article lead you to believe?
   - a. There are more men than women in professional jobs.
   - b. The Brontë sisters thought that they were men.
   - c. England's training school for nurses was in Ohio.

8. Why couldn't women become teachers easily?
   - a. Most women wanted to be nurses instead.
   - b. Most colleges were open only to men.
   - c. They had to work in the business world.

9. Think about the concept for this group of articles. Which statement seems true both for the article and for the concept?
   - a. The typewriter was invented at Oberlin College.
   - b. All women in England are doctors and lawyers.
   - c. People's ideas about women's work have changed.

The "Wish Book"

At the turn of the century, American people often did their shopping from catalogs. A catalog was a book which described in detail the merchandise a shopper could purchase from a certain company. A person could look through a catalog and find everything from men's overalls to coffee grinders. When the shopper decided what to buy, the order was sent by mail. The company delivered the merchandise the same way—by mail.

The catalog offered a handy way of shopping at a time when most people lived in small towns or on farms. In those days, a shopper might have to travel a long distance by horse and buggy to get to the nearest store. After 1918, however, the automobile had been invented. More people were living in cities. Most people could do their shopping directly in a department store. In many areas, catalog shopping disappeared.

A surprising thing has happened in recent years, however. Catalog shopping is popular again. Major companies send out 50 to 60 million catalogs every year. One company has printed its ads in a catalog called the "Wish Book." In it, a person is supposed to find any wished-for item. The "Wish Book" contains some items that would not have been listed in a catalog fifty years ago. Using the "Wish Book," a shopper can purchase a mink coat, an airplane, or even a suit of armor!

Today, both city people and farm people enjoy shopping from catalogs. Catalogs allow them to see pictured merchandise at home at their convenience. They avoid traffic jams and waiting in line. They also save time. The old-fashioned catalog has become the modern shopper's helper.

FIND THE ANSWERS

1. Long ago, a person had to travel
   - a. to get a catalog.
   - b. by horse and buggy.
   - c. to mail orders.
   - d. to find a coffee grinder.

2. The word in paragraph 1 that means *buy* is _____ .

3. The words "old-fashioned" in the last paragraph describe the

   _____ .

4. While it is not directly stated, the article suggest that
   - a. traveling by horse and buggy was fun.
   - b. people buy a lot of suits of armor.
   - c. shopping by catalog can be a good idea.

5. One catalog is called
   - a. the "Wish Book."
   - b. the "Phone Book."
   - c. the "Want Book."

6. On the whole, the article tells about
   - a. shopping from catalogs.
   - b. strange things people buy.
   - c. people's coats.

7. Which statement does the article lead you to believe?
   - a. Catalog shopping will never be popular.
   - b. Airplanes can only be bought from catalogs.
   - c. People can buy almost anything through the mail.

8. Why do city people and farm people enjoy shopping from catalogs?
   - a. It is the law.
   - b. It is convenient.
   - c. They like traffic.

9. Think about the concept for this group of articles. Which statement seems true both for the article and for the concept?
   - a. People are old-fashioned in their ideas.
   - b. People should not avoid traffic jams.
   - c. People sometimes make an old idea modern.

Russia's Cupboard

Once Russia sent criminals and political troublemakers to Siberia. Today, some of Russia's top scientists, technicians, and skilled workers go there. They are trying to tap Siberia's vast natural resources.

Siberia lies in northern Asia, east of the Ural Mountains. It is larger than the United States, but only a small part of it can be used for growing crops. Even there, the soil is poor and the growing season is very short.

In northern Siberia, bone-chilling winds sweep down from the North Pole. The temperature drops to -94° Fahrenheit. It is a land of dark forests, frozen swamps, and icy rivers that flow north to the Arctic Ocean.

Though Siberia's climate is harsh, Russians have long called Siberia "the cupboard" of the country. This is because of its natural resources. Siberia's plains and mountains contain vast amounts of coal, iron, gold, silver, oil, and gas. Siberia's rivers can provide electricity. Its forests can be turned into cellulose products and building materials.

Siberia's industrial production today is thirty times more than it was in 1940. Though Siberia is still uncrowded, it now has more than thirty towns with populations over 100,000. Recently, a 1,900-mile railway across part of Siberia was completed.

Russians once called Siberia "the house of the dead." That is because very few of the criminals and political exiles who were sent there returned alive. But today, Russians no longer think of Siberia as the "the house of the dead." They consider Siberia the nation's future, an area to be prized because of its rich natural resources.

1. Siberia is east of the
    a. Rocky Mountains.   c. Alps.
    b. Ural Mountains.   d. Andes.

2. The word in paragraph 4 that means *supply* or *give* is _____.

3. The words "that flow north to the Arctic Ocean" in paragraph 3 describe the icy
    _____.

4. While it is not directly stated, the article suggests that
    a. scientists today want to go to Siberia.
    b. Siberia is famous for its fine soil.
    c. the summers are very long in Siberia.

5. Siberia has vast reserves of
    a. libraries and schools.
    b. oil and natural gas.
    c. fine soil for farming.

6. On the whole, the article tells about
    a. the temperature in the Arctic.
    b. changes going on in Siberia.
    c. the many criminals in Russia.

7. Which statement does the article lead you to believe?
    a. Siberia is much smaller than the United States.
    b. Siberia's population is growing.
    c. Everybody in Russia wants to live in Siberia.

8. Why is Siberia prized today?
    a. It has rich natural resources.
    b. Russians like its slow rivers.
    c. It has a big house for dead people.

9. Think about the concept for this group of articles. Which statement seems true
    both for the article and for the concept?
    a. Russia hid its valuable minerals in Siberia.
    b. All inhospitable lands have much gold and oil.
    c. Siberia today is not what it seemed long ago.

Wetlands, Wildlife, and Wells

Swamps are level areas where shallow water stands all or most of the year. When the first settlers came to America, there were many more swamps than there are today. To farmers, wetland was wasted land. Ditches were dug to permit the water to drain out of the swamps. As soon as the soil dried, it was plowed and planted.

Some farmland gained in this way was valuable, but much of it was useless for growing crops. It was not until the swamps were nearly all gone that people began to realize how valuable they were.

Swamps were the homes of wild ducks and other birds valued both for sport and as a source of food. Swamp animals such as the muskrat were prized for their fur. When the swamps were drained, these forms of wildlife vanished from large areas of the United States.

The level of underground water was also affected. It dropped lower. Springs ceased to flow, and wells went dry. Only in recent years have people recognized how important swamps are in maintaining the level of ground water.

Much of the water that falls to earth as rain runs quickly into creeks and rivers. This water keeps moving toward the ocean, and little of it soaks down to underground reservoirs. In swampy places, water stands still. It has time to seep down through layers of soil or rock, to be stored there until it is needed.

Farmers build ponds to hold back surface water and give it time to seep down into the earth. Hunters and conservationists are fighting for those swamps and wetlands that still remain. They want to preserve them for wildlife.

FIND THE ANSWERS

1. Water stands still
   - a. in most creeks.
   - b. in swampy places.
   - c. in ditches.
   - d. in rivers.

2. The word in paragraph 4 that means *preserving* or *keeping* is

   _____ .

3. The words "where shallow water stands" in paragraph 1 refer to the level

   areas called _____ .

4. While it is not directly stated, the article suggests that
   - a. people did not know much about the land.
   - b. our wildlife can only live in swamps.
   - c. swamps are not much good for anything.

5. Water from creeks and rivers
   - a. moves toward the ocean.
   - b. falls to the earth.
   - c. makes wells run dry.

6. On the whole, the article tells about
   - a. the level of underground water.
   - b. the need to save our wetlands.
   - c. people who hunt wildlife.

7. Which statement does the article lead you to believe?
   - a. We do not need more underground water.
   - b. Water comes in too many layers.
   - c. Farmers are learning more about the land.

8. Why was farmland from swamps not too valuable?
   - a. It was too wet for the wild ducks and other birds.
   - b. Much of it was useless for growing crops.
   - c. Farmers didn't know how to plow through the water.

9. Think about the concept for this group of articles. Which statement seems true
   both for the article and for the concept?
   - a. Many people now fight to save the wetlands.
   - b. There is too much rain in swampy places.
   - c. Swamp animals are of no importance to people.

1½ BILLION YEARS

The Old, Old Earth

How old is the earth? The ancient Babylonians believed that the earth was 2 million years old. They were more correct than some people who lived much later.

In 1650, an Irish archbishop named James Ussher stated that the world was created at 9:00 A.M. on Sunday, October 23, in 4004 B.C. Ussher based this date on his studies of the Bible and other ancient writings. His statement was printed in a number of books and was accepted by many other scholars.

There were no geologists in Ussher's time. It was only in the 1700s that people began to look carefully at the earth's crust and understand what they saw. They began to realize that whole mountain ranges had been worn down by wind and water. Deep valleys had been carved by running streams. The sea was salty because minerals had been dissolved out of the land.

By 1800, geologists were certain the earth's surface had been greatly changed by slow forces. They estimated that the earth was probably more than 10 million years old. By 1900, geologists changed that figure to 100 million years. One person who helped change people's ideas about the age of the earth was Charles Darwin. He proved that living creatures had changed, very slowly, over long periods of time.

In modern times, new evidence has shown that the earth's age must be measured in billions, rather than millions, of years. Radioactive dating of rocks has proved that some parts of the earth's crust are 2 billion years old. Astronomers, comparing the earth to the sun and some stars, estimate that the earth is 4 to 5 billion years old. Today, most scientists accept this estimate.

FIND THE ANSWERS

1. The age of the earth must be measured in
   a. hundreds of years.
   b. thousands of years.
   c. billions of years.
   d. months and years.

2. The word in paragraph 4 that means *judged* or *counted* is

   _____ .

3. The words "an Irish archbishop" in paragraph 2 describe _____

   _____ .

4. While it is not directly stated, the article suggests that
   a. there have always been geologists.
   b. Charles Darwin changed the animals.
   c. scientists still learn about the earth.

5. Charles Darwin changed people's ideas
   a. about the age of the earth.
   b. about how old they were.
   c. about the dates on the rocks.

6. On the whole, the article tells about
   a. the minerals that made the sea salty.
   b. estimating the age of the earth.
   c. an Irish archbishop named Ussher.

7. Which statement does the article lead you to believe?
   a. We do not have an exact date for the creation of the earth.
   b. The surface of the earth changed only in the year 1650.
   c. James Ussher was born on October 23 in 4004 B.C.

8. Why didn't geologists question the archbishop's statement?
   a. There were no geologists in Ussher's time.
   b. The geologists were all afraid of Ussher.
   c. The geologists thought Ussher was right.

9. Think about the concept for this group of articles. Which statement seems true both for the article and for the concept?
   a. Whole mountain ranges were looked at on October 23.
   b. James Ussher did not want to read the Bible to scientists.
   c. Scientists kept changing their estimates of the earth's age.

Digging for Answers

Why do scientists dig into soil and rock to find the remains of humans and animals? They are seeking answers to strange problems.

In the Middle Ages, people wondered about the odd patterns and markings they sometimes found in rocks. Many believed these markings were the writings of underground spirits. Some thought these rocks had magical power. Others called them "freaks of nature." Some naturalists even expained that the rocks were the bones of strange beasts in legends, such as the unicorn.

We know now that these rocks are not magical or the writing of spirits. They are fossils. Fossils are the remains of once-living animals or plants, or the traces of bones, shells, or leaves preserved in hard minerals.

The first great scientist to study fossils was Georges Cuvier (zhôrzh kü' vē ā'), a French naturalist who lived from 1769 to 1832. Cuvier had already studied living animals and classified them according to similar body parts. When he turned to the study of prehistoric animals, he faced two difficult questions. Why were many animals known from their fossils no longer living? Why were some kinds of fossils found in one rock layer, while quite different kinds of fossils were found in another layer?

From his studies, Cuvier decided that life had changed in great sudden upheavals. Later scientists found signs that made them feel that most changes happened slowly.

A very old story tells about a time when the walls of the ancient city of Jericho fell down. In 1952, Kathleen Mary Kenyon, a British archeologist, led a group of scientists to dig in this 10,000-year-old city in Jordon. They found that the walls had been destroyed and rebuilt at least seventeen times.

FIND THE ANSWERS

1. Cuvier was
   - a. an English scientist.
   - b. a French naturalist.
   - c. a Spanish explorer.
   - d. a Greek historian.

2. The word in paragraph 3 that means *saved a long time* is

   _____.

3. The words "a British archeologist" in paragraph 6 describe

   _____   _____.

4. While it is not directly stated, the article suggests that
   - a. all people are middle aged.
   - b. the unicorn was a real animal.
   - c. people once believed in magic.

5. The archeologist learned that the walls of Jericho fell
   - a. only once.
   - b. every year.
   - c. at least seventeen times.

6. On the whole, the article tells about
   - a. freaks of nature.
   - b. underground spirits.
   - c. the people who seek answers.

7. Which statement does the article lead you to believe?
   - a. People knew a lot in the Middle Ages.
   - b. There have been many ideas about life on earth.
   - c. All strange beasts in legends were unicorns.

8. Why do people dig for the remains of ancient life?
   - a. Everybody likes to get dirty now and then.
   - b. People want to learn more about life on earth.
   - c. It is a good way to find great wealth.

9. Think about the concept for this group of articles. Which statement seems true both for the article and for the concept?
   - a. People now want scientific explanations for things.
   - b. Rocks with magical powers came from unicorns in legends.
   - c. All fossils were found between the years 1769 and 1832.

The Difficult Question

Science, as we think of it, was born when the Greek philosopher Thales (thā′ lēz) of Miletus (mī lē′ təs) (about 640-546 B.C.) asked a difficult question: What makes up our universe?

No one had a ready answer, so Thales went on studying the earth around him, the sky, and the stars. He saw so much water on earth and water falling from the sky as rain that he decided water must be the basic substance of the universe.

Other Greek thinkers became interested in this question. They suggested other answers. One said that because air lies all around the earth, it must be air that makes up all things. Another said that fire, appearing in different forms, was the building block of the universe.

The great Greek philosopher Aristotle lived from 384 to 322 B.C. By Aristotle's time most Greeks had decided that four substances— water, air, earth, and fire—made up the universe. Aristotle believed that these four things could be altered to change into each other. He also thought there might be a fifth substance, different from the others and somehow more perfect, making up the stars and the universe outside of the earth.

The Greek philosophers were feeling their way toward the ideas on which chemistry is based. Centuries later, scientists proved that the universe is made up of certain basic substances. But the list is much more complicated than the Greeks realized. We now know of 103 basic substances which we call "elements."

Although the Greeks knew about gold, silver, copper, carbon, and sulfur, they did not recognize these substances as true elements. They thought fire was an element. We know that fire is a chemical change taking place before our eyes. They thought air and water were elements. We know that they are combinations of elements.

FIND THE ANSWERS

1. Scientists proved that the universe is made up of
   a. certain kinds of water.
   b. true and false elements.
   c. certain basic substances.
   d. water, air, and chemicals.

2. The word in paragraph 5 that means *not simple* is

   _____ .

3. The words "which we call 'elements'" in paragraph 5 describe the 103 basic

   _____ .

4. While it is not directly stated, the article suggests that
   a. Thales asked too many questions.
   b. all Greeks were philosophers.
   c. science began long ago.

5. Thales decided that the basic substance of the universe was
   a. the sky.
   b. stars.
   c. water.

6. On the whole, the article tells about
   a. early attempts to understand our universe.
   b. two thinkers of ancient Greece.
   c. water falling from the sky.

7. Which statement does the article lead you to believe?
   a. Elements cannot be combined with each other.
   b. Some early Greek thinkers were brilliant people.
   c. Nothing ever changes in the universe.

8. Why is our list of basic substances more complicated than Aristotle's?
   a. We now know of 103 basic substances.
   b. Scientists only used Greek lists.
   c. We now have four different substances.

9. Think about the concept for this group of articles. Which statement seems true both for the article and for the concept?
   a. The ancient Greeks refused to recognize gold or silver as elements.
   b. The early Greeks made building blocks of gold for the universe.
   c. Aristotle saw the universe as more complicated than Thales did.

Searching the Skies

For thousands of years, scientists have wondered about the specks of light in the night sky. In A.D. 125, Ptolemy, a Greek astronomer living in Egypt, claimed that the planets and the sun moved around Earth. Though other astronomers had different ideas, Ptolemy's theory was accepted for almost 1,500 years.

In 1543, the Polish astronomer Nicholas Copernicus published a book that explained how Earth and the other planets revolve around the sun. In the early 1600s, Galileo proved that Copernicus was right. Galileo made his observations using a telescope. He was the first astronomer to use one.

Today, astronomers use telescopes that are much more powerful than Galileo's. In 1990, the Hubble Space Telescope began to orbit Earth. The Hubble telescope studies ultraviolet rays, infrared rays, and X-rays from distant stars and galaxies. These are rays that never reach Earth, because they are stopped by Earth's atmosphere. The Hubble telescope has found evidence of a black hole—a collapsed star that absorbs all matter that comes near it. The Hubble telescope has also sent back information about some very young stars.

To study planets in our solar system, scientists have launched unmanned space probes. In 1997, the *Pathfinder* mission landed a small vehicle named

SOJOURNER

Sojourner on Mars. So far, *Sojourner* has learned that the composition of Mars is more like Earth than scientists had thought. Like Earth, Mars has a molten core. Pressure bubbles up from that core and sometimes causes volcanoes.

Though we have already learned much, there are more plans to study the sky. In 2000 and 2001, the *Ulysses* will study the sun. In 2004, the *Cassini* will arrive at the planet Saturn. Then, for 130 days, *Cassini* will pass through Jupiter's tail, which is an energy field that trails Jupiter. As a result of these probes, scientists' ideas about the planets will probably continue to change.

FIND THE ANSWERS

1. The first astronomer to use a telescope was
    a. Ptolemy.
    b. Copernicus.
    c. Hubble.
    d. Galileo.

2. The word in paragraph 1 that means *idea about the way things work* is

    _____.

3. The words "collapsed star" in paragraph 3 describe a _____

    _____.

4. While it is not directly stated, the article suggests that
    a. the telescope was invented sometime around A.D. 125.
    b. the telescope was invented sometime around A.D. 1600.
    c. the telescope was invented sometime around A.D. 1990.

5. The astronomer Galileo
    a. proved that Copernicus was right.
    b. proved that Ptolemy was right.
    c. proved that Mars is like Earth.

6. On the whole, the article tells about
    a. what Jupiter's tail is like.
    b. how to use a telescope.
    c. how people study the planets and stars.

7. Which statement does the article lead you to believe?
    a. Astronauts will soon arrive on Jupiter.
    b. Astronomers know answers about everything.
    c. As time goes on, we know more about planets.

8. Why was the Hubble telescope put in space instead of used on Earth?
    a. In space, it is closer to the stars.
    b. In space, it can detect rays that do not reach Earth.
    c. In space, it cannot be damaged by air pollution.

9. Think about the concept for this group of articles. Which statement seems true for both the article and the concept?
    a. As we learn more, we often change our ideas about things.
    b. After *Sojourner* is finished, we will know everything about Mars.
    c. Our ideas about the planets and stars never change very much.

Great Sports

In the 1932 Olympics, American women won a sweep of gold medals. Wilma Rudolph, a fast-as-lightning black runner, won three gold medals. That same year Babe Didrickson won two gold medals in javelin throwing and hurdling. She also became famous for track. From 1945 to 1950 this incredible athlete won honors for golf.

It is hard to believe that when the Olympics began two thousand years ago, women could not even watch the games. Later, when Romans took charge of the Olympics, women were allowed to compete—but only in the chariot races!

In our times, women not only compete, but they also become wealthy from their athletic skills. Sonja Henie, the famous Norwegian figure skater, won Olympic titles in 1928, 1932, and 1936. Later she made millions of dollars skating in ice shows and movies. Peggy

Fleming, an American, became Olympic figure skating champion in 1968. The next year she earned nearly a million dollars skating in movies and for TV.

Fortunes are being made by women in other sports as well. Tennis queen Billie Jean King was the first woman to earn more than $100,000 in prize money in one year—1971. Twenty-five years later, Steffi Graf led all women in tennis earnings, winning more than $2,500,000. That same year, Karrie Webb became the first woman in golf to earn more than a million dollars in a year.

Professional sports continue to open up to women. In 1969, women jockeys entered horse racing. In 1976, Janet Guthrie and Arlene Hiss began competing in stock car races. During the 1990s, a professional baseball team and two professional basketball leagues for women were started and have attracted thousands of fans.

FIND THE ANSWERS

1. Babe Didrickson and Wilma Rudolph
   a. liked to walk after lunch.
   b. won gold medals in the Olympics.
   c. always slept before they ran.
   d. wished they could be in the Olympics.

2. The word in paragraph 2 that means *a two-wheeled carriage* is

   _____.

3. The words "Olympic figure skating champion in 1968" in paragraph 3 describe

   _____ _____.

4. While it is not directly stated, the article suggests that
   a. Romans thought women could never learn to swim.
   b. women seldom like to compete in the Olympics.
   c. women would like to enter new sports.

5. The first woman tennis player to earn over $100,000 in a year was
   a. Sonja Henie.
   b. Wilma Rudolph.
   c. Billie Jean King.

6. On the whole, the article tells about
   a. more and more women taking part in sports.
   b. women who do better things than playing games.
   c. women who like running because they find it fun.

7. Which statement does the article lead you to believe?
   a. Women can never win stock-car races.
   b. Basketball is harmful for girls.
   c. Prize money for women in sports is rising.

8. Why do women want to compete in the Olympics?
   a. They like to have their pictures taken.
   b. Their friends at home are proud of them.
   c. They enjoy the challenge and the chance to become famous.

9. Think about the concept for this group of articles. Which statement seems true both for the article and for the concept?
   a. The ancient Greeks thought women should only watch the Olympics.
   b. Some people never change their minds about anything.
   c. Sports fans are becoming more and more interested in women athletes.

The Long Fight

Slavery has existed, in one form or another, in most periods of history. But few people thought that it was wrong until one small group began to speak out strongly against it.

Soon after the first slave traders carried African captives to America, the Quakers in England took a stand opposing slavery. Their long fight began in 1671. There were few slaves in England, then or later, but slave labor was used in the British colonies. Many slave traders were English people who made a profit from slavery.

The Quakers did not believe in violence, so they carried on a peaceful fight. Their chief weapons were the pen and the printing press. Quakers and their friends published many books and papers that described the misery aboard slave ships and on plantations. At an early date, the Quakers freed all the slaves they themselves owned.

Little by little, public opinion in England began to move toward the Quaker viewpoint. People began to see that slavery was wrong. They began to demand new laws that would make slavery illegal.

In 1807, more than 100 years after the fight began, the anti-slavery forces won their first major victory. Parliament passed a law ending the slave trade. In 1833, another law freed all slaves in British colonies, and paid slave-owners for their losses.

Laws ending slavery were not passed until the people demanded them. And the people did not demand the laws until they were convinced that slavery must be ended.

In America, too, Quakers took the lead in the antislavery movement. But in America, the slave question was not settled by law. The long fight started by a peaceful people ended in a bloody war.

88

1. Quakers did not believe in
    a. history.   c. peace.
    b. violence.   d. laws.

2. The word in paragraph 4 that means *against the law* is _____.

3. The words "that described the misery aboard slave ships" in paragraph 3

   describe the many _____ and _____.

4. While it is not directly stated, the article suggests that
    a. Quakers do not know how to fight.
    b. England passed a law against Quakers.
    c. there is more than one way to fight.

5. The fight against slavery really began
    a. in England.
    b. in America.
    c. in sixteenth-century Europe.

6. On the whole, the article tells about
    a. Quakers who became slaves.
    b. the fight against slavery.
    c. the first slave traders.

7. Which statement does the article lead you to believe?
    a. Words can be used as weapons.
    b. Quakers sold printing presses.
    c. Slave owners were not paid.

8. Why did it take so long for laws to be passed against slavery?
    a. Quakers would not free any slaves.
    b. People had to fight the Quakers.
    c. People did not demand the laws.

9. Think about the concept for this group of articles. Which statement seems true both for the article and for the concept?
    a. There were no slaves in ancient times.
    b. Today, most people dislike the idea of slavery.
    c. Quakers were the first slave traders.

America's Own Music

Folk music is a special kind of music. It springs from the life of ordinary people. It was learned by ear, rather than from notes written down on paper. It was kept alive in the memories of singers who passed the songs on to others. Until fairly recently, many musicans did not think of this as music at all.

In the 1700s and 1800s, American musicians studied under European-trained teachers. These musicians played music by European composers. Some were unhappy that their own country had not given the world any great composers or a new musical style. If they knew of America's great wealth of folk music, they thought it beneath their notice.

All around them, untrained voices were raised in song. American Indians had lullabies and war chants. American Negroes had work songs and religious spirituals. Cowhands had special story-telling ballads that they sang around their lonely campfires. In the mountains of Virginia and North Carolina, Americans of English descent sang tunes that dated back to Shakespeare's time.

In 1892, a well-known Czech composer and conductor named Anton Dvořák (an' ton dvôr' zhäk) came to the United States. He stayed three years. Impressed by the expressive Indian and Negro folk tunes and the new rhythms he heard, Dvořák wrote a symphony in which he tried to echo their spirit. He was one of the first composers to write classical music that reflected native American music.

After 1900, some composers finally began to study American folk music. They wrote symphonies, operas, and ballets that actually used native American melodies. American musicians discovered at last the rich American music that many Americans already knew and loved.

FIND THE ANSWERS

1. Around their campfires, cowhands sang
   - a. lullabies.
   - b. war chants.
   - c. religious spirituals.
   - d. story-telling ballads.

2. The word in paragraph 4 that means *moved deeply* is _____.

3. The words "that dated back to Shakespeare's time" in paragraph 3 refer to

   _____ .

4. While it is not directly stated, the article suggests that
   - a. many people have heard folk music sung.
   - b. Shakespeare wrote folk music for Americans.
   - c. only Czech composers can play folk music.

5. Some composers have used native American melodies in
   - a. tunes for people like Shakespeare.
   - b. letters to European musicians.
   - c. symphonies, operas, and ballets.

6. On the whole, the article tells about
   - a. a Czech composer.
   - b. America's folk music.
   - c. life in the 1800s.

7. Which statement does the article lead you to believe?
   - a. American folk music came from many people.
   - b. American Indians gave us our folk music.
   - c. Americans of English descent should not sing.

8. Why did European-trained musicians only play European music?
   - a. American folk music was not allowed to be played.
   - b. They didn't know how to play American folk music.
   - c. They thought folk music was beneath their notice.

9. Think about the concept for this group of articles. Which statement seems true both for the article and for the concept?
   - a. Folk music is very hard to play or sing.
   - b. Musicians today appreciate many kinds of music.
   - c. All American music comes from Europe.

The "Why" Stories

In ancient times, people wondered about the stars, about the movement of the sun across the sky, about the change of seasons. They could not explain these things, and so they made up stories about them. These myths, or "why" stories, developed in many parts of the world.

The ancient Greeks told about Demeter (di mē′ tər), the goddess of agriculture, who kept the earth green all year. One day her daughter Persephone (pər sef′ ə nē) was kidnapped by Hades, god of the dead. Demeter was so unhappy that she let everything on earth die. At last, Hades agreed to permit Persephone to return to her mother for part of the year. During that period, everything on earth flourished again. One season, however, Persephone had to remain with Hades. During that season, the earth stayed cold and bare. So winter was explained.

American Indians told of an old woman who stood on a high mountain. When the moon was full, she cut off bits of it and flung these bits about the sky. This explained where the stars came from, and why the moon became small.

The Indonesians told of gods who lived in mountains. When the gods were angry, they threw out fire and molten rock. When they were sad, their sighs rose like plumes of smoke. This explained volcanoes.

Hundreds of legends like these were passed by word of mouth from one generation to another. Among some people, the "why" stories grew long and complicated and finally became part of their religion. Later, these stories were put in books.

We do not read "why" stories today for explanation of natural wonders. We read them for enjoyment and because they help us understand people of other lands and times.

FIND THE ANSWERS

1. Demeter was the Greek goddess of
   - a. the Indians.
   - b. agriculture.
   - c. volcanoes.
   - d. the underworld.

2. The word in paragraph 2 that means *grew well* is

   _____ .

3. The words "of other lands and times" in paragraph 6 describe the

   _____ .

4. While it is not directly stated, the article suggests that
   - a. the Indonesian gods were better than the Greek gods.
   - b. all old people stand on high mountains in America.
   - c. people have had a great need to understand their world.

5. The ancient Greeks explained why we have
   - a. a winter season.
   - b. Indonesian gods.
   - c. volcanoes.

6. On the whole, the article tells about
   - a. the unhappy ancient Greeks.
   - b. Indonesians who live on mountains.
   - c. the way myths and legends began.

7. Which statement does the article lead you to believe?
   - a. Legends were not passed on to each generation.
   - b. The Indonesian gods kidnapped Persephone.
   - c. Different people had different ideas about things.

8. Why did early humans make up myths?
   - a. They were trying to explain the things around them.
   - b. They wanted to keep the angry gods happy.
   - c. They were afraid Demeter would bring more winter.

9. Think about the concept for this group of articles. Which statement seems true both for the article and for the concept?
   - a. All of the "why" stories are short and simple.
   - b. Science, not myth, explains natural wonders today.
   - c. No one bothers to read the old "why" stories now.

The Auto Haters

In 1896, there were just two automobiles in Detroit, and the police set a speed limit of five miles per hour for them. One of the two automobiles belonged to Henry Ford, who designed and built it himself. It had bicycle-type wheels and was steered with a tiller, or lever.

When Mr. Ford took his auto out for a spin, a friend on a bicycle went ahead to warn buggy drivers to get their horses under control.

From the first, autos caused problems for horses, and horse owners caused problems for auto owners. The noise and odd appearance of the new vehicles frightened all but the calmest horses. The animals were likely to rear up on their hind legs and then run madly in any direction. Buggies and carriages were wrecked. Often people riding in them were thrown out and injured.

There were little more than 300 automobiles in the United States in 1896, but thousands of people owned and drove horses. It was hardly surprising that laws were passed which favored the horse over the auto. Some cities would not permit autos on their streets at all, while others allowed people to drive autos only at night or on certain streets. St. Louis charged a toll of $10, a large sum in that day, for the privilege of driving an auto through the city.

In some places, auto haters took the law into their own hands. They placed broken glass, tacks, and barbed wire on roads to damage auto tires.

In time, attitudes changed. By 1916, just twenty years after Henry Ford built his first auto, Americans were buying 1½ million cars a year. Today, the horse has disappeared from American streets and highways.

1. In Detroit in 1896, there were just two
   a. buggy drivers.   c policemen.
   b. bicycles.   d. automobiles.

2. The word in paragraph 4 that means *allow* is _____ .

3. The words "which favored the horse over the auto" in paragraph 4 refer to

   _____ .

4. While it is not directly stated, the article suggests that
   a. people would still rather have horses than autos.
   b. horses disappeared as soon as they saw Henry Ford.
   c. it did not take long for autos to become popular.

5. Henry Ford steered his first car
   a. with a tiller.
   b. with a pump.
   c. with a horse.

6. On the whole, the article tells about
   a. what a large sum of money $10 used to be.
   b. police officers who lived in St. Louis and Detroit.
   c. the attitude of people toward the first autos.

7. Which statement does the article lead you to believe?
   a. Horses were only allowed on the streets at night.
   b. It cost Mr. Ford $10 to live in St. Louis.
   c. The auto haters failed to stop the new autos.

8. Why did Mr. Ford's friend warn buggy drivers that a car was coming?
   a. Cars frightened the horses.
   b. He was afraid of Mr. Ford.
   c. Police officers made him do this.

9. Think about the concept for this group of articles. Which statement seems true both for the article and for the concept?
   a. Henry Ford owned the only bicycle.
   b. People learn to accept new ideas.
   c. Everybody should own a horse today.

The Auto That Won

The automobile was not the invention of only one person. A number of different people in different countries, took to the roads in self-propelled vehicles in the 1800s. Their "horseless carriages" were not only different in appearance but used different kinds of energy.

One group of inventors used steam engines. Another group preferred electric batteries. Still another group experimented with the newly invented internal-combustion engine. Each kind of power had both its good points and its bad points.

"Steam carriages" carried passengers on regular routes in England as early as 1829. At one time 100 different companies were manufacturing steam autos in the United States. The Stanley Steamer, manufactured from 1897 to 1929, was one of the most popular makes. Steam autos were fast and powerful but noisy. In addition, many people were fearful of an engine that required an open fire and hot steam to run.

The first electric auto was driven in England in 1874. By 1900, there were more electric autos in use in the United States than any other kind. Electrics were quiet and easy to operate, but they couldn't go very fast and their batteries had to be recharged after about forty miles.

A Frenchman named Jean Lenoir invented the internal-combusion engine in 1860, and in 1863 he built and drove his own auto. Since gasoline was not yet available, Lenoir used illuminating gas as fuel. In 1893 and 1894, the Duryea brothers and Elwood Haynes built America's first autos with internal-combustion engines.

The first gasoline-powered autos were slow, undependable, and difficult to start, but the engines were soon improved. After a while, the manufacturers who built this kind of car won the automobile market. Steamers and electric cars disappeared from the highways for many years.

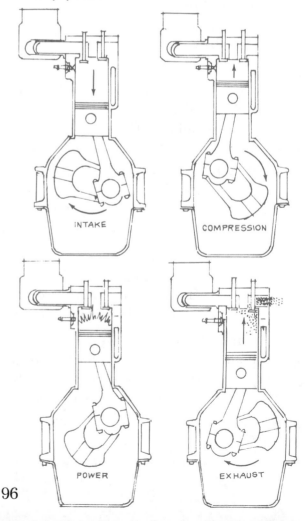

INTAKE COMPRESSION

POWER EXHAUST

FIND THE ANSWERS

1. One of the most popular steam autos in the United States was
   - a. the Lenoir engine.
   - b. the Haynes auto.
   - c. the English carriage.
   - d. the Stanley Steamer.

2. The word in paragraph 3 that means *needed* is _____.

3. The words "that required an open fire and hot steam to run" in paragraph 3 describe an _____.

4. While it is not directly stated, the article suggests that
   - a. the best way to run an engine is with an open fire.
   - b. it was relaxing to drive electric automobiles.
   - c. all steamcars were run with illuminating gasoline.

5. Steam autos were fast and powerful
   - a. but hot.
   - b. and quiet.
   - c. but noisy.

6. On the whole, the article tells about
   - a. different powered autos.
   - b. a Frenchman who used gas.
   - c. routes used in England.

7. Which statement does the article lead you to believe?
   - a. Electric autos were too fast to be used.
   - b. The first automobiles were the best ones.
   - c. Electric cars were clean cars to operate.

8. Why did Lenoir use illuminating gas?
   - a. He was afraid of internal combustion.
   - b. He liked it more than electricity.
   - c. Gasoline was not yet available.

9. Think about the concept for this group of articles. Which statement seems true both for the article and for the concept?
   - a. Inventions are improved upon as time goes by.
   - b. Lenoir borrowed an electric car.
   - c. Only one person invented the automobile.

Loki and the Magic Apples

Asgard (äs' gärd) was the home of the Norse gods. Odin (ō' din), father of all gods, lived there, as did Odin's brother, Honir (hō' nēr). Loki (lō' kē), the Fire-god, also called Asgard his home, but Loki was not really a god. He was a mischievous and evil creature related to the Giant race. However, Loki had grown tired of his own people and had come to Asgard to serve the gods.

One day Odin, Honir, and Loki were visiting earth. They wandered across the land until evening came. Then Loki said, "I am so hungry. Can we stop to eat?"

Odin laughed. "Fetch one of the animals from that herd of cattle," he said, "and we will roast it for our supper."

Hunger lent speed to Loki's feet. Before long, the gods were sitting before a fire watching meat turn on a spit.

"It must be ready," Odin said, his mouth watering for the food. Loki took some meat from the fire. The meat was raw!

"The fire is not hot enough," Honir cried. Loki threw more logs on the fire, but still the meat did not brown.

"There is great evil here," Odin said. As soon as the words were spoken, the still of the night was shattered by a scream of laughter. Looking up, the gods saw a tremendous eagle watching them.

"The meat will stay raw unless I

98

get a good part of it," the eagle said.

"Agreed," Odin said immediately. "But make haste. We are all starving." At once the fire blazed again, and this time the meat was done within a few minutes. The eagle swooped down and seized great chunks of meat in his claws and beak.

"Greedy creature!" Loki shouted, offended at the amount of meat the bird took. He snatched a large stick from the ground and beat the eagle across the back. The stick stuck to the eagle, and Loki stuck to the stick. Off went the eagle, dragging the unhappy Loki across the rough ground.

"Mercy!" Loki pleaded. "Release me, and I promise you shall have all the meat."

The eagle, who was really Thiassi (tē äs′ i), the Giant of Winter, said, "I do not want your meat. I want the goddess Iduna (ē dün′ ə) and her magic apples of Youth. You must get her for me. If you do not, I will drag you across the earth until you are destroyed."

"Great Thiassi," Loki said, for he knew now who the eagle was. "The gods would kill me if anything happened to Iduna. Her magic apples keep the gods young. They would never permit Iduna to leave Asgard."

"Then die!" Thiassi snarled.

"I do not want to die," Loki grumbled. "I will do as you wish."

At once the giant eagle brought Loki back, dropped him at Odin's feet, and flew off. Loki did not tell the gods what had happened. But Odin suspected that the eagle was one of the giant race in disguise. He said nothing, however, for he thought the eagle had punished Loki for leaving his own people.

Back in Asgard, Loki went directly to Iduna. "I have seen apples exactly like the ones you carry in your golden basket," Loki lied. "They grow in a grove of trees on earth."

"You must take me there," Iduna cried.

As soon as Iduna entered the grove, her golden basket of apples swinging from her arm, Thiassi swooped down. He carried Iduna to the frozen land of the Giants, where he dropped his eagle disguise.

"Marry me," he begged, "and feed me magic apples that I may be like the gods."

But Iduna refused. As long as she did not offer the apples freely, their magic could not work, no matter how Thiassi raged.

In Asgard, meanwhile, the gods began to age. Even the great Odin grew gray and wrinkled.

"Where can Iduna be?" the gods wondered. Loki, who knew all, said nothing. At last, a messenger sent by Odin to search the world returned.

"Iduna lives in Thiassi's castle in the land of the Giants," the messenger said.

Odin stared at Loki thoughtfully. "Thiassi, the Giant of Winter who disguises himself as an eagle. Perhaps the same eagle who dragged

Loki away and then returned him to us?"

"He threatened to kill me," Loki wailed.

"If you wish to live," Odin said grimly, "you will find a way to bring Iduna back."

Loki thought and thought. At last he said, "Give me the magic cloak which permits its wearer to assume any shape. With it on, I can become a falcon and fly to Thiassi's castle."

The cloak was given to Loki, who flew immediately to the frozen land of the Giants. He darted in through the highest window of Thiassi's castle into the small room where Iduna sat. Loki turned Iduna into a sparrow. Taking her up gently in his claw, he began the flight back to Asgard.

They had gone a little way when Loki discovered that the eagle was pursuing them. Loki sped faster. In Asgard, the gods could see the falcon with the tiny sparrow chased by the raging eagle. They built a fire and waited. Soon, in a last desperate spurt of speed, Loki crossed the border into Asgard. The eagle was so close that he could not stop or turn back. The fires, at a signal from Odin, leaped up and destroyed the giant bird.

The gods turned to welcome Iduna, who stood before them once more in her own form. She gave them the magic apples to eat, and soon the gods were young and strong again.

As for Loki, the gods soon forgave him. They did not realize that as long as the mischievous Fire-god lived among them, there would always be trouble in Asgard.

956 words

III

The Same Ideas Are Seen in Different Ways by Different Groups

In this section, you will read about many different ways of looking at the same things. You will read about this in the areas of history, biology, economics, anthropology, geography, Earth science, space, political science, art, and engineering.

Keep these questions in mind when you are reading.

1. Why do all people not agree on the same idea?

2. Is it good to have different ideas? Why?

3. Should we know more than our own point of view?

4. Why is this helpful or harmful?

5. Are you willing to listen to the ideas of others?

Look on pages 8-10 for help with words you don't understand in this section.

The Fence War

When the great herds of bison had been killed and the Native Americans subdued, ranchers took over the western plains. Open range land stretched from Texas north to Montana, most of it owned by the government and all of it unfenced. The ranchers turned their cattle loose to graze where they pleased.

Cattle raising was an important industry in Texas as early as 1840. Some ranchers became the richest people in the West. Like royalty, they became used to ruling the land. Then the first farmers arrived. Ranchers had nothing but contempt for these newcomers, whom they called "nesters." The nesters were homesteaders who built cabins, plowed fields, planted crops, and enclosed their land with fences. The homesteaders brought with them rolls of the newly invented barbed wire that they used to build inex-

pensive but cattleproof fences. Most homesteaders settled along creeks and rivers, often at places where ranchers had been watering their herds. With barbed wire fences surrounding the new farms, range cattle were unable to reach water.

Both ranchers and homesteaders felt very strongly about the proper use of the land. To the homesteaders, the range was good farm country. To the ranchers, the range was obviously cattle country and only cattle country. Feelings between the two groups ran high. Ranchers threatened the homesteaders, and vice versa. Sometimes threats were carried out. People on both sides were shot and killed in this "war" over the land.

In 1885, Congress finally passed a law that gave certain areas of the range to the homesteaders and other areas to the ranchers.

1. Range cattle could not reach water because of
   - a. barbed wire fences.
   - b. cabins and crops.
   - c. buffalo.
   - d. Native Americans.

2. The word in paragraph 1 that means *overcome by force* is
   _____.

3. The words "from Texas north to Montana" in paragraph 1 describe the open range _____.

4. While it is not directly stated, the article suggests that
   - a. ranchers were better than the homesteaders.
   - b. ranchers and homesteaders were good friends.
   - c. ranchers were used to having their own way.

5. Cattle raising was an important industry in
   - a. Maine.
   - b. Texas.
   - c. Ohio.

6. On the whole, the article tells about
   - a. building inexpensive barbed wire fences.
   - b. great herds of bison taken by ranchers.
   - c. the fight between ranchers and homesteaders.

7. Which statement does the article lead you to believe?
   - a. A war can sometimes be settled by law.
   - b. Range cattle did not really need water.
   - c. Barbed wire was invented by ranchers.

8. Why did the ranchers leave the land unfenced?
   - a. They wanted the cattle to graze freely.
   - b. They wanted the nesters to grow crops.
   - c. They thought the farmers liked it better.

9. Think about the concept for this group of articles. Which statement seems true both for the article and the concept?
   - a. Each group saw a different use for the land.
   - b. Nesters were birds that lived with the farmers.
   - c. Homesteaders soon became cattle owners.

When Horses Pulled Boats

Between the years 1800 and 1850, settlers streamed westward over the Allegheny Mountains. Farms and cities appeared in the new land that became the states of Ohio and Indiana.

With settlement came the need for better transportation. Farmers wanted to buy plows, saws, and other manufactured goods from the East. They needed to ship their farm products to eastern markets.

At first, most people were excited about having a system of canals connecting the Great Lakes with navigable rivers. They knew New York State's Erie Canal had quickly paid for itself, and that it had brought prosperity to cities along its route.

Between 1825 and 1840, the new states plunged into the building of canals. Work was begun on three long canals that were to connect Lake Erie with cities on the Ohio River. Two canals were planned in Ohio and one in Indiana.

In the same years these canals were started, America's first railroads were being built in the eastern states. Some people began to be enthusiastic about the idea of a network of rail lines, rather than canals, crisscrossing Ohio and Indiana. They believed the new steam locomotives would be able to pull trains faster than horses could pull canal boats. They knew that railroads could be used in winter when the canals froze and canal boats stood idle. Soon, new companies were organized to build railroads west of the Alleghenies.

Both systems of transportation were used in Ohio and Indiana between 1830 and 1860. By 1870 it was clear that the railroads could offer superior service. The canals fell into disuse before they earned money enough to pay for their construction.

FIND THE ANSWERS

1. At first most people were excited about
   - a. the Allegheny Mountains.
   - b. navigable rivers.
   - c. horses and buggies.
   - d. a system of canals.

2. The word in paragraph 3 that means *money* or *fortune* is

   _____ .

3. The words "that were to connect Lake Erie with cities on the Ohio River" in

   paragraph 4 describe three long _____ .

4. While it is not directly stated, the article suggests that
   - a. all navigable rivers connect with the Great Lakes.
   - b. the railroads put some people out of business.
   - c. none of the new states wanted to build any canals.

5. Railroads offered
   - a. superior service.
   - b. to buy plows and saws.
   - c. money for canals.

6. On the whole, the article tells about
   - a. farm products in the East.
   - b. Indiana and Lake Erie.
   - c. canals and railroads.

7. Which statement does the article lead you to believe?
   - a. Most people do not need transportation.
   - b. Farmers buy a lot of locomotives.
   - c. Some things go out of date very quickly.

8. Why was the Erie Canal a good canal?
   - a. It had no cities along its route.
   - b. It quickly paid for itself.
   - c. It made work for railroads.

9. Think about the concept for this group of articles. Which statement seems true both for the article and for the concept?
   - a. Some people liked canals better than railroads.
   - b. Water in the canals never froze in the winter.
   - c. Ohio and Indiana refused to use railroads.

Which Is It—Animal or Plant?

It is generally easy to separate the many forms of life we know about into two large groups, the animal kingdom and the plant kingdom. But there are some living things that do not fit neatly into either category. One such living thing is called *Euglena* (ū glē′ nə).

Some botanists claim Euglena as a plant. In certain biology textbooks, Euglena is listed with the one-celled plants called algae. Some zoologists claim Euglena as an animal. In many biology textbooks, Euglena is listed with the one-celled animals called protozoans. Which is it—animal or plant?

What is the difference between a plant and an animal? An animal is a living thing that can move about. It feeds on plants, or on other animals, or both, but it cannot manufacture its own food.

A plant is a living thing that cannot move about. Most plants contain chlorophyll. This is the green coloring matter which can use energy absorbed from sunlight to manufacture the food plants need.

Euglena is a tiny organism that floats in stagnant ponds. It seems to fit equally well in either the animal kingdom or the plant kingdom. It can swim about. It can feed on plant and animal matter in the water, but it can also manufacture its own food. And it is green!

To solve the problem of where to fit Euglena, some scientists have set up a new classification. They say one-celled animals and one-celled plants, though very much like each other, are quite different from the many-celled, more complex forms of life. Therefore these scientists place most one-celled organisms together with a few other more complex forms of life into a special group. They call this group *protista*.

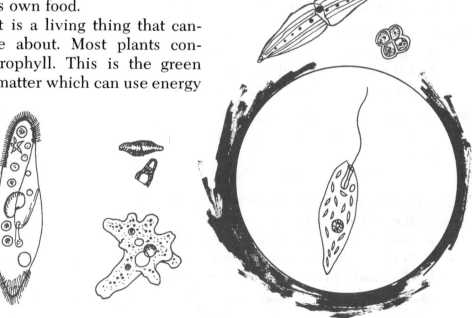

106

FIND THE ANSWERS

1. Some scientists have set up
   - a. some new organisms.
   - b. a new classification.
   - c. some odd forms of life.
   - d. some old problems.

2. The word in paragraph 1 that means *class* or *group* is _____.

3. The words "that floats in stagnant ponds" in paragraph 5 describe the tiny organism called _____.

4. While it is not directly stated, the article suggests that
   - a. some forms of life are still puzzling.
   - b. plants can move about like animals.
   - c. most scientists don't like plants.

5. Euglena is an organism that
   - a. turns green in textbooks.
   - b. floats in stagnant ponds.
   - c. feeds on many scientists.

6. On the whole, the article tells about
   - a. a one-celled organism.
   - b. manufacturing food.
   - c. biology textbooks.

7. Which statement does the article lead you to believe?
   - a. There are quite a few one-celled organisms.
   - b. Euglena is the only one-celled organism.
   - c. One-celled organisms do not belong together.

8. Why is Euglena like a plant?
   - a. It can manufacture its own food.
   - b. It can solve problems for scientists.
   - c. It can color the sunlight red.

9. Think about the concept for this group of articles. Which statement seems true both for the article and for the concept?
   - a. Stagnant ponds have fresh water.
   - b. All animals are turning green.
   - c. Scientists do not always agree.

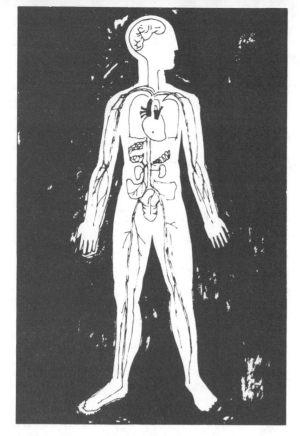

The Oozing Heart

In the second century A.D., a famous Greek physician named Galen (gā′ lən) claimed life came from three kinds of spirits. "Natural" spirits were found in the liver. "Animal" spirits were found in the brain. "Vital" spirits were found in the heart. Galen also believed there were two different kinds of blood in the body. One kind moved in and out of the arteries. Another kind moved in and out of the veins. Both moved in some slow, irregular way and oozed through the central wall of the heart.

Fifteen centuries later, doctors still accepted Galen's ideas. They explained heartbeats by saying that these were caused by the expansion of the "vital spirits" inside the heart.

In 1628, an English doctor named William Harvey published a book full of new ideas. Heartbeats, he said, were not caused by the expansion of vital spirits. The heart was a pump. Each heartbeat was a muscular contraction that forced about two ounces, or one-fourth cup, of blood from the heart.

At that rate, the heart pumped 1,500 gallons of blood a day! How could the body manufacture so much blood, doctors asked. Where did it all come from? Where did it all go? A grown human body contains only about 5½ quarts of blood. Harvey explained this blood was circulated through the body and returned to the heart again and again.

These new ideas shocked many doctors. Medical scientists were divided. A school of medicine in Paris led the group that opposed Harvey's ideas. Some doctors in other countries took Harvey's side in the fight. But Harvey did not live to see his ideas as fully accepted as they are today.

Things are different now. Today, most doctors welcome new ideas.

1. Galen believed life came from
    a. 1,500 gallons of blood.
    b. three kinds of spirits.
    c. oozing blood.
    d. the arteries.

2. The word in paragraph 2 that means *spreading* or *enlarging* is

   _____.

3. The words "full of new ideas" in paragraph 3 describe a _____ published by William Harvey.

4. While it is not directly stated, the article suggests that
    a. Galen did not know too much about the body.
    b. other people's ideas should not be questioned.
    c. William Harvey was a famous Greek physician.

5. A grown human body contains about
    a. 1,500 gallons of blood.
    b. 5½ quarts of blood.
    c. 2 ounces of blood.

6. On the whole, the article tells about
    a. the death of Dr. William Harvey.
    b. the spirits found in the liver.
    c. different ideas about the body.

7. Which statement does the article lead you to believe?
    a. William Harvey had no right to publish a book in 1628.
    b. William Harvey pumped 1,500 gallons of blood a day.
    c. William Harvey's book changed some doctors' ideas.

8. Why isn't a heartbeat caused by vital spirits?
    a. Vital spirits are only found in the brain.
    b. A heartbeat is a muscular contraction.
    c. A grown man's body has no room for vital spirits.

9. Think about the concept for this group of articles. Which statement seems true both for the article and for the concept?
    a. No one should be asked to accept a new idea.
    b. It is hard for some people to change their minds.
    c. Ideas in the medical world can never be changed.

A Matter of Choice

In Europe, small cars have always been more popular than large cars. In the United States, large cars and midsize cars are more popular than smaller cars. As a result, European automakers used to make a wider variety of compact cars while American automakers used to build bigger, heavier cars. However, these days, automakers in both America and Europe produce cars of different sizes. This is because most automakers export their cars all over the world.

The price of gasoline is one reason for differences in automobile preferences. Since gasoline is more expensive in Europe, many Europeans want smaller, lighter cars that will travel a long way on a gallon of gas. This increased gas mileage makes the cars more economical to run.

Other reasons also enter into the big or little car decision. Many Old World cities have narrow, winding streets. In these cities a small car is easier to handle than a large one.

For a long time, few Americans bought compact cars. Instead they chose large cars, because these roomy cars were more comfortable for large families and long trips. Some people also liked the powerful engines that large cars had. Since gasoline was cheap, drivers did not mind that the large cars used a lot of gas.

But in the 1970s, there were gas shortages in the United States. The price of gas went up. Though large cars were still more popular than smaller cars, sales of small cars that used less gas increased. Some people also bought small cars because these cars caused less air pollution than larger cars.

Today, Americans' car preferences are still changing. Though Americans are still buying many small cars, the fastest growing sales are for certain kinds of large cars. These types of cars are called minivans and sport utility vehicles. They are very popular today. But of course, that could change tomorrow.

FIND THE ANSWERS

1. Old World cities often have
   - a. heavier cars.
   - b. less gasoline.
   - c. narrow, winding streets.
   - d. no air pollution.

2. The word in paragraph 1 that means *small* is _____.

3. The words "more comfortable for large families" in paragraph 4 describe the _____.

4. While it is not directly stated, the article suggests that
   - a. no large cars are sold in Europe.
   - b. small cars are not expensive to run.
   - c. most Americans buy European cars.

5. In the 1970s
   - a. European cars finally came to United States.
   - b. there were gas shortages in the United States.
   - c. people in the United States stopped buying small cars.

6. On the whole, the article tells about
   - a. driving in cities.
   - b. big cars and small cars.
   - c. how the price of gasoline changes.

7. Which statement does the article lead you to believe?
   - a. European car companies sell many cars in America.
   - b. Utility vehicles are small cars.
   - c. Minivans are becoming less popular.

8. In the 1970s, why did sales of smaller cars increase?
   - a. There was less air pollution.
   - b. There was a new kind of small car, called the minivan.
   - c. The price of gas went up.

9. Think of the concept for this group of articles. Which statement seems true for both the article and for the concept?
   - a. The price of gasoline cannot be predicted.
   - b. People like to have a variety of cars to choose among.
   - c. Small cars are better than large cars.

A Room Full of Gold

The captured Inca king stood on tiptoe and reached as high as he could. A Spanish soldier painted a line around the wall at that point. It was nine feet from the floor. Atahualpa (at′ə wäl′ pə), the Inca prisoner, had been placed in this 17-by 22-foot room by the Spanish explorer Pizarro. Now, to secure his freedom, Atahualpa promised Pizarro to fill the room with gold up to the painted line.

Soon incredible amounts of treasure were brought from the royal storehouses. There were no gold coins, but there were dishes, cups, and chairs fashioned from the yellow metal. There were panels that had once covered whole walls. There were such objects as stalks of corn and life-sized animals, all beautifully wrought of pure gold.

When the room was finally filled, the Spaniards valued the golden hoard at 20 million dollars. But what was its value to the Incas, who now gladly gave it to ransom their king?

The Incas did not use gold for trading. In fact, there was no kind of money in the Inca civilization, and almost no ownership of property. All gold belonged to the rulers, whose artisans turned it into objects of great beauty. If Indian farmers found gold, they gave it to the Inca ruler as a gift. Gold had no value for them, for they could not eat it or even use it to buy things they needed. The Incas could not understand the greed of the Spanish soldiers for this metal of so little value to them.

Atahualpa did not survive his imprisonment. He died at the hands of the foreign conquerors, who destroyed a civilization and priceless art objects for gold.

FIND THE ANSWERS

1. The Inca king was taken prisoner by the
   a. Americans.
   b. Indians.
   c. Spanish.
   d. English.

2. The word in paragraph 1 that means *make certain* is _____.

3. The words "that had once covered whole walls" in paragraph 2 describe the

   _____.

4. While it is not directly stated, the article suggests that
   a. all Incas walked around on tiptoe.
   b. most Indian farmers planted gold on their land.
   c. the Spanish treated the Incas very badly.

5. The Inca king promised to fill the room with gold
   a. up to the painted line.
   b. all the way to the ceiling.
   c. as high as a soldier.

6. On the whole, the article tells about
   a. the importance of farming.
   b. the ransoming of an Inca king.
   c. the size of an Inca room.

7. Which statement does the article lead you to believe?
   a. The Spanish freed the Inca prisoner.
   b. The Spanish saved the Inca civilization.
   c. The Spanish did not care about the Incas.

8. Why did the Indian farmers give gold to their ruler?
   a. It was too beautiful for them.
   b. It had no value for them.
   c. They didn't like its color.

9. Think about the concept for this group of articles. Which statement seems true both for the article and for the concept?
   a. There was too much money in the Inca civilization.
   b. The Incas were puzzled by Spanish greed for gold.
   c. Artisans turned gold into food for the farmers.

113

Clothing Talks

When you wear something, you are often saying, "Look at me!" Your clothing communicates to the world what you want the world to think of you. For example, when you go on a job interview, you might choose clothes that make you seem dependable. When you go to a party, you might choose clothes that make you look exciting.

In different civilizations at different times, different kinds of clothes have been acceptable. In Scotland and parts of the Orient, men as well as women wore skirts. In Turkey and China and among the Inuit, both men and women wore trousers. But in ancient Greece, men who wore trousers were thought to be savages. In the United States today, both men and women wear pants.

Over the centuries, anthropologists have learned, the clothing people wore was related to the position they held in society. In most civilizations, important people donned special clothing and headgear to show their authority. In the eighteenth century, kings and queens wore special clothing, often elaborately made and difficult to keep clean. Since poor people could not afford to wear this kind of clothing, it became a symbol of wealth.

Today some people still wear clothing that symbolizes their position in life. Sometimes clothing clearly shows the organization that a person works for. Postal workers, airline attendants, and some factory workers wear uniforms. Others wear expensive clothes that indicate their status as wealthy people.

Now many teenagers and adults buy clothes from a specific designer or company. They may like the reputation of the designer or the company and want to share that reputation. But one basic reason for choosing clothes is the same as it has always been. People choose their clothes to tell others who they are and what they like.

FIND THE ANSWERS

1. Greeks thought men who wore trousers were
    a. anthropologists.
    b. very wealthy.
    c. Inuit.
    d. savages.

2. The word in paragraph 3 that means *persons who study society* is

    _____.

3. The words "that symbolizes their position in life" in paragraph 4 describe the
    _____ that some people wear.

4. While it is not directly stated, the article suggests that
    a. there was no special clothing for kings and chiefs.
    b. only rich, important people lived in the eighteenth century.
    c. the clothes people wore depended on where they lived.

5. Some people wear clothing that symbolizes
    a. where to find service stations.
    b. where jewelry is sold.
    c. their position in life.

6. On the whole, the article tells about
    a. clothing worn by both men and women.
    b. the way to show who has authority.
    c. people who got rich in the twentieth century.

7. Which statement does the article lead you to believe?
    a. People who belong to organizations must wear uniforms.
    b. Each new period brings some change in clothing.
    c. People might not look attractive in new clothes.

8. Why do some people buy clothes from a specific designer?
    a. They work for the designer.
    b. They like the designer's reputation.
    c. They think that it makes it easier to choose clothes.

9. Think about the concept for this group of articles. Which statement seems true
    both for the article and for the concept?
    a. Most people enjoy wearing some special kinds of clothing.
    b. Airlines do not allow factory workers to wear uniforms.
    c. All restaurant workers wear bright clothes at home.

115

Never on Friday

What do you eat? Who you are and where you live usually determine the answer.

In the Arctic, fish and meat are the only foods available. Eskimos cannot raise fruit or vegetables. In the tropics, the plants supply much of the food people eat.

American children drink milk from cows, but children of Bedouin herders in the Arabian desert drink milk from camels. In Tibet, milk comes from yaks, but in Lapland children grow strong on milk from reindeer. Indian herders in the Andes Mountains in South America give their children milk from llamas. In some parts of the world, children never see or taste milk.

Buddhists eat no meat for they believe that every living creature has a soul which may reappear someday in human form. Hindus are not allowed to eat beef, but some Hindus eat no meat at all. Moslems and Orthodox Jews eat no pork. For centuries, Catholics ate no meat on Fridays. Religious beliefs and customs make the difference in these eating habits.

Some people do not eat meat because they do not believe in killing animals for food. They are called vegetarians.

Many foods are associated with certain countries. Fish and chips is a food from England. Everyone knows the small sausage so popular in the United States, although it may be called by different names. It is the hot dog, frankfurter, red hot, or wiener. A President of the United States once served hot dogs to the visiting king and queen of England because they wanted to taste this American "delicacy"!

As climates, beliefs, and customs vary, so do the foods that people eat.

1. In England, many people eat
   a. thin, flat pancakes.
   b. tropical vegetables.
   c. fish and chips.
   d. milk from camels.

2. The word in paragraph 1 that means *decide* is _____ .

3. The words "so popular in the United States" in paragraph 6 describe the

   small _____ .

4. While it is not directly stated, the article suggests that
   a. people around the world believe milk is good for children.
   b. milk only comes from camels.
   c. children always drink milk everywhere in the world.

5. Some people who do not eat meat are called
   a. orthodox.
   b. vegetarians.
   c. herders.

6. On the whole, the article tells about
   a. herds in the Andes Mountains.
   b. eating meat on Friday.
   c. food habits in many places.

7. Which statement does the article lead you to believe?
   a. There are many reasons behind certain food habits.
   b. For centuries, Catholics went hungry on Fridays.
   c. Buddists do not eat meat because they are Hindus.

8. Why do Eskimos eat fish and meat?
   a. They cannot raise fruit or vegetables.
   b. They are orthodox vegetarians.
   c. They do not like milk from camels.

9. Think about the concept for this group of articles. Which statement seems true
   both for the article and for the concept?
   a. Buddhists eat many tortillas on Friday.
   b. All people do not like the same food.
   c. Kings and queens visiting America must eat red hots.

Cattle or Wildebeest?

There are two kinds of ranches in Africa. One kind raises cattle like those on European farms and American ranches. The other kind has native African animals, such as the wildebeest and the zebra. Both kinds of ranches are in the same business. They produce meat for people to eat.

English and German settlers raised cattle successfully in the highlands of East Africa. This land was somewhat like the lands they had left in Europe. But in other parts of East and Central Africa, cattle ranchers did not do as well. Cattle ranchers had to change the land to make it fit the needs of their livestock. They had to dig wells, for the European-type animals need more water to drink than native African animals do. Often cattle ranchers had to bring in seed, for the imported animals refused to eat many of the African plants.

Game ranchers, on the other hand, keep livestock that is well suited to the land, its climate, and its plant life. Native animals are not bothered by diseases and insect pests that often kill imported cattle. Furthermore, when the meat of wild animals is properly processed, it is as tender and tasty as beef.

Game ranchers and cattle ranchers still do not agree on which kind of ranching is best suited to the land. Settlers from Europe like to use the land as they used it in their home countries. They feel that game ranching prevents the development of the land. Game ranchers think it is wrong to try to adapt the land to the cattle. They are convinced it is wiser to use animals already adapted to the land.

1. The wildebeest is a native
   a. German animal. c. European animal.
   b. American animal. d. African animal

2. The word in paragraph 2 that means *brought in* is _____.

3. The words "such as the wildebeest and the zebra" in paragraph 1 describe native African _____.

4. While it is not directly stated, the article suggests that
   a. all early ranches were run by German settlers.
   b. ranches are important in Africa.
   c. imported animals do well in Africa.

5. In some places, cattle ranchers had to
   a. agree with game ranchers.
   b. change their livestock.
   c. dig wells and bring in seeds.

6. On the whole, the article tells about
   a. two kinds of ranching in Africa.
   b. European cattle called wildebeests.
   c. animals and plants native to Africa.

7. Which statement does the article lead you to believe?
   a. The land of Africa is not suited for ranching.
   b. There is no room in Africa for people who disagree.
   c. Both kinds of ranchers are right in some ways.

8. Why don't game ranchers adapt the land to cattle?
   a. They want to raise native animals on African land.
   b. They think no one can change the land.
   c. They want the settlers to adapt to African ways.

9. Think about the concept for this group of articles. Which statement seems true for both the article and the concept?
   a. Some people can never agree about certain things.
   b. The production of meat is not important.
   c. All cattle ranchers do very well in Africa.

Land Turned Upside Down

A flat bed of coal up to six feet thick lies hidden under the surface of the land in southwestern Indiana. Mine owners claim the best way to remove this coal is by strip mining.

Strip mining is done by giant power shovels that dig deep trenches to expose the coal. In this process of digging, topsoil moves to the bottom. Broken rock and barren subsoil move to the surface. The land is actually being turned upside down. The power shovels deposit tons of earth in cone-shaped hills or steep-sided ridges. When the digging is over, a deep trench usually remains unfilled. After a while, such trenches begin to form deep, narrow lakes from water that flows in from under the ground. Some of these lakes are as much as a mile long.

Many people oppose strip mining. They say it destroys the beauty of the land and much of its usefulness. Mine owners agree this is true. But strip mining, they say, gives work to local citizens and helps pay taxes that support local schools. Much of the coal goes to nearby electric-generating plants. This helps keep the price of electric power lower than it would be otherwise.

In 1977, a federal law was passed that required mine owners to reclaim strip mines. This means that when the owners have finished with the mines, they must return the land to its original condition. As a result of the law, about 2.5 million acres of recently closed mines have been reclaimed.

More than 100,000 acres of older mines have also been reclaimed. Like the newer mines, these reclaimed mine sites are being used in many ways. Some strip mines that formed lakes have been stocked with fish and become public parks. Other mines have been converted into farms, pastures, campgrounds, and golf courses.

1. Strip mining is done by
   a. picks and shovels.
   b. giant power shovels.
   c. powerful giants.
   d. cones on hills.

2. The word in paragraph 1 that means *say positively* is _____.

3. The words "under the surface of the land" in paragraph 1 describe a flat bed of _____.

4. While it is not directly stated, the article suggests that
   a. all coal is in Indiana.
   b. coal cannot be mined.
   c. people still need coal.

5. Some strip-mine lakes are now
   a. campgrounds.
   b. generating plants.
   c. in local schools.

6. On the whole, the article tells about
   a. local people who pay taxes for their schools.
   b. strip mining and how it changes the land.
   c. the price of electric power in Indiana.

7. Which statement does the article lead you to believe?
   a. Fish will not stay in strip-mine lakes.
   b. The 1977 federal law has improved the look and usefulness of the land.
   c. It is impossible to convert stripped land into parks.

8. Why do some people oppose strip mining?
   a. It destroys the beauty of the land.
   b. It is too expensive.
   c. It is against the law.

9. Think about the concept for this group of articles. Which statement seems true both for the article and for the concept?
   a. All wildlife reserves are made from strip mines.
   b. People take different sides about strip mining.
   c. Strip mining does not change the land very much.

The Mystery of "Drift"

In the early 1800s, many people were studying rocks and guessing at the earth's history. They were beginning to understand how volcanoes, wind, and the action of running water had changed the crust of the earth.

In many parts of northern Europe, pioneer geologists found gravel mixed with pebbles and rocks of different sizes. This loose material was piled on top of the ground. Where did it come from? What had moved it? Geologists decided that water must have washed the loose material up into piles during some great flood. They called this loose, unsorted material "drift."

In the late 1830s, a very different explanation was presented by Louis Agassiz (ag′ ə sē). He was not a geologist but a zoologist whose chief field of study was fossil fishes. Agassiz came from Switzerland, and he had climbed over Alpine glaciers. He had observed their slow but powerful movement and had noted how the glaciers carried broken rocks along with them.

Agassiz was the first to suggest that at one time most of northern Europe had been covered by a giant sheet of ice. It was this continental glacier, he said, that deposited "drift."

At first, many scientists refused to accept the idea of an ice age or glacial drift. They suggested Agassiz go back to his fossil fishes and leave geology to the experts. They continued to believe and teach the older ideas.

But other scientists in both Europe and America were impressed by Agassiz's theory. When they began searching for evidence of an ancient ice age, they found proof that Agassiz's theory was correct.

FIND THE ANSWERS

1. The crust of the earth was changed by
   a. people who studied the rocks.   c. pioneer geologists.
   b. volcanoes, wind, and water.   d. pebbles and rocks.

2. The word in paragraph 6 that means *proof* is _____.

3. The words "whose chief field of study was fossil fishes" in paragraph 3

   describe Louis Agassiz, who was a _____.

4. While it is not directly stated, the article suggests that
   a. early geologists knew all the answers.
   b. early geologists were puzzled by "drift."
   c. there was too much loose material in Europe.

5. Some scientists began searching
   a. for glaciers carrying broken rocks.
   b. for a giant sheet of ice over Europe.
   c. for evidence of an ancient ice age.

6. On the whole, the article tells about
   a. a scientist who climbed Alpine glaciers.
   b. the ideas scientists had about "drift."
   c. the way running water changed the earth.

7. Which statement does the article lead you to believe?
   a. Scientists must try to prove their theories.
   b. All the scientists believed Agassiz was wrong.
   c. Ice had nothing to do with shaping the earth.

8. Why did scientists search for evidence of an ice age?
   a. They wanted proof that the theory was correct.
   b. They all liked Agassiz and wanted to help him.
   c. They wanted to impress all of their friends.

9. Think about the concept for this group of articles. Which statement seems true
   both for the article and for the concept?
   a. Scientists always agree with one another.
   b. People in the same field may often disagree.
   c. Old ideas are always better than new ideas.

The Argument

The history of the earth is written in its rocks, but people did not begin to "read the rocks" carefully until the eighteenth century. Then mining became a growing industry in northwestern Europe. People digging into the crust of the earth uncovered layers of different kinds of rock. What was the explanation for these layers?

Between 1775 and 1817, Abraham Werner, a professor in Germany, taught his students that continents, mountains, and rocks had all been produced by the action of water. Once a great ocean had covered the world, Werner said. As the water receded, layers of rock formed from minerals in the water. Granite, the oldest rock in the earth's crust, had appeared first. Other kinds of rocks appeared as the seas receded. Werner believed the earth would never change again. Werner and those who agreed with him were called Neptunists, after Neptune, Greek god of the sea.

In Scotland, Dr. James Hutton (1726–1797) took a wide interest in

many fields of science. Hutton believed that water had helped but had not been the only force in forming the continents. Rivers, Hutton thought, carried soil and rock material with them as they flowed into the sea. Then the heat beneath the earth's surface made this material fuse and expand. Finally, the material once carried to the sea by the rivers emerged to form islands, mountains, and even continents. The world had been shaped slowly, he said. It had been undergoing changes for centuries and would continue to change. Hutton and his followers were called Plutonists, after the ancient god of the fiery underworld, Pluto.

Today, Hutton is often called the creator of modern geology. During his lifetime, however, arguments flared often between the Neptunists and the Plutonists. Both schools studied the same evidence found beneath their feet. But both saw the same thing in different ways.

FIND THE ANSWERS

1. Hutton today is often called the creator of modern
   - a. geology.
   - b. history.
   - c. biography.
   - d. zoology.

2. The word in paragraph 3 that means *spread out* or *get bigger* is

   _____ .

3. The words "the oldest rock in the earth's crust" in paragraph 2 describe

   _____ .

4. While it is not directly stated, the article suggests that
   - a. the early Greek gods were great scientists.
   - b. it is not possible for the earth to change.
   - c. not much was known about the earth long ago.

5. Hutton thought that heat below the earth's surface
   - a. made undersea rock materials expand.
   - b. made Pluto god of the underworld.
   - c. made an ocean cover the whole world.

6. On the whole, the article tells about
   - a. a growing industry in Europe.
   - b. layers of rocks and minerals.
   - c. the different ideas about the earth.

7. Which statement does the article lead you to believe?
   - a. People do not always understand the things they see.
   - b. It is wrong for two groups to study the same thing.
   - c. Dr. James Hutton was not very interested in science.

8. Why did the Neptunists and the Plutonists disagree?
   - a. They thought one Greek god was better than another.
   - b. They both saw the same thing in different ways.
   - c. They didn't want their professors to get along.

9. Think about the concept for this group of articles. Which statement seems true both for the article and for the concept?
   - a. Students in different countries learned different things.
   - b. Abraham Werner wanted to be called the creator of geology.
   - c. Dr. James Hutton was a professor who taught in Germany.

A Bagful of Nothing

When the great comet of 1682 appeared, people were afraid. They said the strange light in the sky warned of evil things to come. Few believed Edmond Halley, an English astronomer who said the comet was a natural body following a set path around the sun.

The same comet, Halley said, had been in the sky in 1607, and would return in 1758, 1835, and 1910. Halley died in 1742. He did not live to see his prediction come true, but the comet did return in those years. Halley's Comet, as it is now called, swings around the sun and then far out through space in a long orbit. The round trip is approximately seventy-six years.

We know now that comets have no light of their own. The bright glow comes from sunlight. Astronomers believe comets may have a hard core,

or nucleus, containing frozen water vapor, solid carbon dioxide, and other gases. Some comets appear to have no nucleus but are made up entirely of gases.

When comets move near the sun, some of the solid matter changes to gas. The gas forms a cloud, or coma, around the nucleus and streams out in a tail. Gas particles in the tail are so light they can be pushed away by sunlight. The tail of a comet always points away from the sun.

Some comets may be millions of miles long, but one famous astronomer, Percival Lowell, has called them a "bagful of nothing." Suppose the earth and a comet collided. The tail might make our sky brighter. A shower of meteors would rain on the earth from the nucleus, but the pieces would burn or melt and vaporize before they hit the earth.

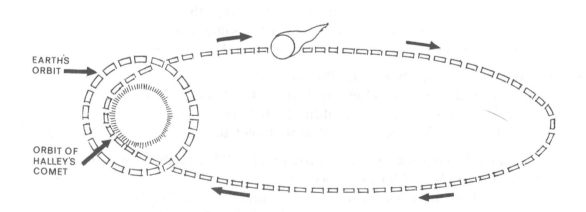

EARTH'S
ORBIT

ORBIT OF
HALLEY'S
COMET

1. The tail of a comet always points
   a. away from the earth.
   b. away from the sun.
   c. toward the moon.
   d. toward other comets.

2. The word in paragraph 5 that means *crashed together* is _____.

3. The words "containing frozen water vapor, solid carbon dioxide, and other gases" in paragraph 3 describe the hard core, or _____, of some comets.

4. While it is not directly stated, the article suggests that
   a. we should be afraid of comets.
   b. showers are caused by comets.
   c. comets cannot hurt the earth.

5. The trip for Halley's Comet is approximately
   a. twenty months.
   b. seventy-six years.
   c. fifteen days.

6. On the whole, the article tells about
   a. strange lights that warn people.
   b. the natural bodies called comets.
   c. one famous astronomer named Lowell.

7. Which statement does the article lead you to believe?
   a. Halley's Comet will return around 1986.
   b. Halley's Comet is too long for us to see.
   c. Halley's Comet will bring evil things.

8. Why can gas particles be pushed away by sunlight?
   a. The particles all point toward the sun.
   b. Gas particles in the tail are very light.
   c. Meteors from the sun freeze the particles.

9. Think about the concept for this group of articles. Which statement seems true both for the article and for the concept?
   a. Edmond Halley was wrong to make predictions.
   b. Ideas about comets have changed over the years.
   c. Percival Lowell calls comets too many names.

The Big Puzzle

Astronomers do not always agree with each other. One thing on which they cannot agree is the origin of the universe. The universe includes millions of galaxies. Each galaxy is made up of billions of stars. Our earth, moon, and sun are part of the same galaxy. We call this galaxy the Milky Way.

No one can tell us exactly how the universe came into being. Astronomers can only give us their theories on the way it began. Guesses based upon serious research and study are called theories.

One such theory is known as the "big bang" theory. It claims that all matter in the universe was made simultaneously as a result of a giant explosion about 10 billion years ago. They say that no new matter has been created since the time when the galaxies were formed.

Other astronomers do not accept the big bang theory. Their idea is called the "steady state" theory. These astronomers believe there was no sudden beginning to the universe just as there will be no sudden end. They say matter has always been created at a constant rate and will go on being created forever. Other people have still other theories, but there is as yet no way of proving or disproving any of them.

Through the use of their instruments, scientists have learned that the galaxies are moving away from each other. Scientists may not be able to agree with each other on how the universe began. But they do agree that the universe is growing. They also admit humans have much to learn before they can solve the puzzle of the universe.

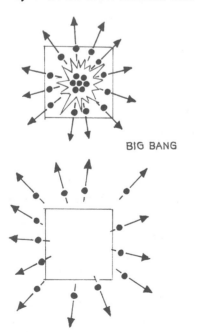

BIG BANG

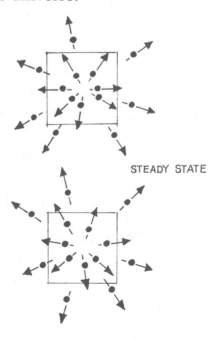

STEADY STATE

FIND THE ANSWERS

1. Scientists agree that the universe
   - a. is growing.
   - b. is getting smaller.
   - c. is not important.
   - d. has too many stars.

2. The word in paragraph 1 that means *beginning* is _____.

3. The words "based upon serious research and study" in paragraph 2 describe

   _____.

4. While it is not directly stated, the article suggests that
   - a. the universe should come to an end at once.
   - b. the universe has too many galaxies in it.
   - c. scientists need instruments in their work.

5. We call our own galaxy
   - a. the Milky Way.
   - b. the only star.
   - c. a giant bang.

6. On the whole, the article tells about
   - a. a good way to prove scientific theories.
   - b. theories about the origin of the universe.
   - c. forcing scientists to agree with each other.

7. Which statement does the article lead you to believe?
   - a. The universe may puzzle people for a long time.
   - b. No one wants to know how the universe began.
   - c. The universe can never puzzle the astronomers.

8. Why can astronomers only give us their theories?
   - a. They don't want people to know the truth.
   - b. They can't tell exactly how the universe began.
   - c. They want to keep this information secret.

9. Think about the concept for this group of articles. Which statement seems true both for the article and for the concept?
   - a. All the galaxies in the universe are called Milky Ways.
   - b. The puzzle of the universe has been solved by scientists.
   - c. Different people have different ideas about the universe.

of its fine name, the new United States was not really united at all. Each state was still like a separate little nation with a government of its own.

The states wanted to go on being separate. But they understood that a central government was needed to do things for the whole nation that each state could not do alone. A central government could provide mail service, pass uniform trade laws, collect taxes. It could make treaties with other countries. And it could help settle arguments between the states themselves.

Delegates from each state met in Philadelphia in 1787 to work out a plan for a central government. These delegates drew up the Constitution, which provided a way of keeping order among the states. It provided the government with the right to make laws, and see that they were obeyed. It even set up a supreme court to make sure that the laws were fair.

The delegates tried to put down clearly just what powers were being given to the new central government. They also decided what rights were to be kept by each state. The delegates, in writing the Constitution, came to an important agreement among themselves about the central government. But many remained in sharp disagreement about the rights of the states. Since that time in the 1700s, many people continue to debate this issue of states' rights.

The Important Agreement

From 1774 to 1789, the colonies were governed by the Continental Congress. It carried on the fight against England until the colonies were free. In 1776, the Continental Congress wrote the Declaration of Independence. Later, it set up some rules for the new nation. But in spite

1. Delegates from each state met in
   a. Peoria.
   b. Pomona.
   c. Philadelphia.
   d. Pittsburgh.

2. The word in paragraph 4 that means *argue* is _____.

3. The words "like a separate little nation" in paragraph 1 describe each

   _____ .

4. While it is not directly stated, the article suggests that
   a. a central government helped all of the states.
   b. the colonies did not need a central government.
   c. people in the central government wore uniforms.

5. A supreme court was set up to make sure
   a. that the laws were passed.
   b. that the laws were fair.
   c. that no one could make laws.

6. On the whole, the article tells about
   a. delegates who kept order in the supreme court.
   b. planning a central government for a new nation.
   c. the writing of the Declaration of Independence.

7. Which statement does the article lead you to believe?
   a. The delegates collected taxes for a new mail service.
   b. The delegates had to work hard to make a new nation.
   c. Only delegates can now settle arguments between states.

8. Why was a central government needed?
   a. It could keep the delegates busy writing.
   b. It could pass laws about uniforms.
   c. It could do things for the whole nation.

9. Think about the concept for this group of articles. Which statement seems true both for the article and for the concept?
   a. A constitution can only be written in Philadelphia.
   b. The delegates were not able to write very clearly.
   c. Some people still feel strongly about states' rights.

The Fair Plan

It would have been easier to write the United States Constitution if, in 1787, all thirteen states had been about the same size. As it was, the large states and the small states disagreed about how they were to be represented in the new central government.

The smaller states naturally wanted all states represented equally, regardless of size. The larger states thought that they should have more representatives than the small states.

Virginia was one of the largest and richest of the states. It was to be expected that the plan Virginia presented at the Constitutional Convention would favor the big states. The Virginia Plan called for a legislature with an upper house and a lower house. It asked that representation in both houses be based on the population and wealth of the individual states.

New Jersey was one of the smallest states. In its plan, New Jersey called for a legislature with only one house in which all states would have the same number of representatives.

There were so many arguments that many delegates to the Convention wanted to forget the whole idea and leave! It seemed for a time that the delegates would never come up with a plan that everyone could agree upon as fair. It was Connecticut that finally came up with a plan that was acceptable to all the states. This plan called for a two-house legislature. In the upper house, or Senate, large and small states would have equal representation and power. In the lower house, or House of Representatives, each state would be represented according to its population.

This plan is still in use. And in both houses, people still have the right to argue for their own ideas.

FIND THE ANSWERS

1. One of the largest and richest states was
   - a. New Jersey.
   - b. Virginia.
   - c. Rhode Island.
   - d. Connecticut.

2. The word in paragraph 3 that means *separate* is

   _____ .

3. The words "with an upper house and a lower house" in paragraph 3 describe

   a _____ .

4. While it is not directly stated, the article suggests that
   - a. all states were exactly the same size.
   - b. the size of a state was important.
   - c. Virginia was one of the small states.

5. Connecticut finally came up with
   - a. some delegates.
   - b. a terrible idea.
   - c. an acceptable plan.

6. On the whole, the article tells about
   - a. the size of the house for some representatives.
   - b. the population in the state of New Jersey.
   - c. deciding on fair representation for the states.

7. Which statement does the article lead you to believe?
   - a. Virginia is still the largest and richest state today.
   - b. The House of Representatives is no longer being used.
   - c. We still think the delegates came up with a good plan.

8. Why did many delegates want to leave the Convention?
   - a. The delegates were very homesick.
   - b. They didn't like Connecticut.
   - c. There were too many arguments.

9. Think about the concept for this group of articles. Which statement seems true both for the article and for the concept?
   - a. The delegates forgot the whole idea and went home.
   - b. Each delegate fought hard for his or her own ideas.
   - c. We no longer use the plans the delegates made.

Art in a Window

There are many forms of art, and they make our lives richer in many ways. Stained glass is the art form most closely connected with religion. Stained glass windows in churches go back to the eleventh century. Windows made about 1100 can still be seen in a cathedral in a city in Germany. In the twelfth century, schools teaching the art of making stained glass windows could be found in many parts of northern Europe.

This tradition of Christian art arose in times when most people could not read. Paintings and stained glass windows were like picture books. They illustrated Bible stories to help people remember what they had been taught.

Christian art was filled with human figures. No human figures ever appeared in Jewish religious art. The second commandment forbidding the making of graven images was understood in Jewish law to mean there could be no picturing of God. Nor could humans be pictured, since they were made in God's image. Synagogues often had beautiful embroidered curtains, floor mosaics, and wall paintings. But these portrayed only religious symbols, such as the seven-branched candlestick described in the Bible.

In the early 1960s, the artist Marc Chagall was asked to design a series of stained glass windows. The windows were for a new synagogue to be built in Jerusalem. Chagall knew he could not use figures to illustrate stories in the Bible. He used emblems to represent the twelve tribes of Israel. Heroes of the Old Testament were symbolized in the form of animals, fish, birds, flowers, and stars.

In cathedrals or synagogues, with or without figures, stained glass windows continue to be an art form many people find very beautiful.

1. Stained glass windows are closely connected
   - a. with embroidered curtains.
   - b. with seven-branched candles.
   - c. with religion.
   - d. with picture books.

2. The word in paragraph 3 that means *carved* is _____ .

3. The words "like picture books" in paragraph 2 describe the

   _____ and stained glass _____ .

4. While it is not directly stated, the article suggests that
   - a. stained glass windows do not go far back in time.
   - b. stained glass windows are only found in Germany.
   - c. stained glass windows can tell different stories.

5. The tradition of Christian art arose at a time when
   - a. schools were teaching art.
   - b. no one was able to see.
   - c. people could not read.

6. On the whole, the article tells about
   - a. floor mosaics and wall paintings.
   - b. the art of stained glass windows.
   - c. famous stories found in the Bible.

7. Which statement does the article lead you to believe?
   - a. Windows are only found in twelfth century schools of art.
   - b. Images are forbidden in all Christian churches today.
   - c. Stained glass windows are only one kind of art form.

8. Why did Marc Chagall use emblems?
   - a. He could not use human figures.
   - b. He could not draw very well.
   - c. He didn't know any Bible stories.

9. Think about the concept for this group of articles. Which statement seems true both for the article and for the concept?
   - a. Christian art has no figures in it.
   - b. People like different art forms.
   - c. Bible stories cannot be illustrated.

The Islands and the Mainland

Long ago a queen named Liliuokalani ruled beautiful Hawaii. In 1959, Hawaii became the fiftieth state in the union. Now no monarch rules these islands two thousand miles from the mainland.

With Congress so far away in Washington, D.C., how do Hawaiians get United States lawmakers to understand their needs? They do this by sending elected representatives to the capital city. These members of Congress make sure that the government understands the way Hawaiians think about taxes, tariffs, and political matters.

Representative Patsy Mink was voted into Congress in 1964. That was the beginning of a congressional career that has lasted more than 30 years. All through her career, Representative Mink showed Congress the peaceful Hawaiian way of getting along with people of all races. Since she believes that all people are equal, she sponsored many bills to help gain human rights and promote racial equality.

Like Representative Mink, Daniel Key Inouye is of Japanese descent. He became the first United States representative from Hawaii in 1959. Then, in 1963, he became one of Hawaii's two U.S. senators. Since then he worked in Congress to help Asians who are very poor. He also worked for improving cities and for ecology.

In 1990, Hawaiians elected Daniel Akaka to complete the term of Senator Spark Matsunaga. Since he is both an Asian American and a native-born Hawaiian, Senator Akaka has an understanding of the needs of Hawaiians.

Along with his colleagues, Daniel Inouye and Patsy Mink, Daniel Akaka studied changing conditions in Hawaii. The three lawmakers sponsored bills to protect Hawaii's tourism, fishing, shipping, and agriculture. As they work in Congress, the people's representatives help the mainland to see things the way the islanders see them.

FIND THE ANSWERS

1. Long ago beautiful Hawaii was ruled by
   - a. strange people.
   - b. a president.
   - c. a queen named Liliuokalani.
   - d. the union.

2. The word in paragraph 1 that means *the ruler of a country* is
   _____.

3. The words "of Japanese descent" in paragraph 4 describe _____.

4. While it is not directly stated, the article suggests that
   - a. few people live in Hawaii.
   - b. tourists seldom visit Hawaii.
   - c. people of any race are welcome in Hawaii.

5. Representative Mink
   - a. has promoted racial equality.
   - b. has worked on education issues.
   - c. hardly ever makes speeches.

6. On the whole, the story tells about
   - a. the history of Hawaii.
   - b. lawmakers who help Congress to understand Hawaiians.
   - c. how Hawaii became the fiftieth state in the union.

7. Which statement does the article lead you to believe?
   - a. Daniel Key Inouye was Hawaii's second member of Congress.
   - b. Perhaps someday Hawaii will have another queen.
   - c. The fiftieth state is proud of the Hawaiian members of Congress.

8. How do tHawaiian lawmakers in Washington know what is going on at home?
   - a. They watch television.
   - b. They read old and new books.
   - c. They study changing conditions in Hawaii.

9. Think about the concept for this group of articles. Which statement seems true both for the article and for the concept?
   - a. Geographical distance can lead to differences of opinion.
   - b. Islanders don't know what laws can be passed in Congress.
   - c. Hawaiians should spend more time on the mainland.

A Key Three Feet Long

How big is the key that unlocks your front door? Is it three feet long? Ridiculous! No one today carries a key that awkward. But there was a period when ancient Greeks did carry curved keys about three feet long. These keys, ornately decorated in gold and silver, were so heavy they had to be carried over the shoulder. They served no real purpose, however, for almost any curved stick, as well as the real key, could open the door.

The ancient Romans used much smaller keys that were so decorative people often wore them on rings. Locks were not set into Roman doors, but were chained on the outside. These locks were also very ornamental.

In India, locks were constructed as part of a puzzle, often in the shape of a bird. The keyhole was usually concealed under one of the bird's wings.

During the Middle Ages, lockmakers built traps into the locks. One lock shot off a gun if anyone tampered with it, while another dropped a sharp blade that cut off the thief's fingers.

Because locks were often easy to pry open, it became a custom in Spain for homeowners to hire someone to watch the block. No one carried a key to any front door. When owners wished to enter their homes, they clapped their hands. The person watching then came and unlocked the door. In some parts of Spain, this old custom is still in force.

Today, most American homes use a lock invented in the 1860s by a portrait painter whose work was little known. His art did not bring him fame, but everyone who uses a Yale lock certainly knows the artist's name!

FIND THE ANSWERS

1. During the Middle Ages, lockmakers built locks
   a. for thieves.   c. with mice.
   b. for Indians.   d. with traps.

2. The word in paragraph 1 that means *hard to handle* is _____.

3. The words "ornately decorated in gold and silver" in paragraph 1 describe

   the _____.

4. While it is not directly stated, the article suggests that
   a. people for centuries have wanted to lock their doors.
   b. it has never been necessary to lock a door in Rome.
   c. all locks on doors today must be decorative.

5. In India, locks were constructed as
   a. traps for birds.
   b. rings on a chain.
   c. part of a puzzle.

6. On the whole, the article tells about
   a. birds who were part of a puzzle.
   b. locks and keys since ancient times.
   c. block watchers who lived in Spain.

7. Which statement does the article lead you to believe?
   a. Ancient people liked decorative things.
   b. There were no thieves in the Middle Ages.
   c. Portrait painters always invent locks.

8. Why were the early Greek keys awkward to carry?
   a. They were three feet long and heavy.
   b. They were hung from the wings of birds.
   c. They were chained to the shoulders.

9. Think about the concept for this group of articles. Which statement seems true both for the article and for the concept?
   a. Locks and keys were different in many countries.
   b. People hide their keys under the wings of birds.
   c. Locks in Spain were hard for thieves to open.

People Movers

The crowded sky has become a serious problem in aviation. But the "crowded ground" is also a growing problem. Airports have become so large it is not possible for passengers to walk everywhere they wish to go.

Engineers in the transportation industry call airplanes "primary people movers." The elevators, escalators, moving sidewalks, and surface vehicles used on the ground are "secondary people movers." The problem of secondary people moving happens anywhere in the world where the big new planes land. Two 747 jet liners and two air buses, for example, may unload 1,300 people and thousands of pieces of baggage into one small area within a five-minute period. Moving them out of the airport quickly is a major puzzle. There are almost as many solutions as there are airports.

At the airport in Geneva, Switzerland, the moving sidewalks are in tunnels. These sidewalks connect different buildings with the main terminal. At Chicago O'Hare International Airport, an underground tunnel connects two concourses of Terminal One. Moving sidewalks take passengers on a 2.5-minute ride through the tunnel. To make the ride interesting, the tunnel includes a neon light sculpture that runs across the ceiling. The sculpture is programmed to provide changing light patterns that go along with music.

For longer distances, many airports use trains. At Denver International Airport, subway trains travel between the main terminal and the airline gates. At O'Hare Airport, automated trains run on elevated tracks. These trains connect the domestic terminal and the international terminal with remote parking lots.

Wherever you go by plane, you will find that engineers are solving the people-moving problem in different and interesting ways.

FIND THE ANSWERS

1. Elevators and escalators are called
   - a. vehicle movers.
   - b. primary people movers.
   - c. secondary people movers.
   - d. monorails.

2. The word in paragraph 4 that means *far off* or *distant* is _____.

3. The words "runs across the ceiling" in paragraph 3 describe the

   _____.

4. While it is not directly stated, the article suggests that
   - a. there is no way to move people from one place to another.
   - b. there are great numbers of people traveling today.
   - c. all airports carry passengers on underground trains.

5. Denver International Airport uses
   - a. subway trains between the main terminal and the airline gates.
   - b. a jet liner between the remote parking lots and airport.
   - c. buses and taxis from one international airport to another.

6. On the whole, the article tells about
   - a. the problem of ground transportation.
   - b. people movers in the crowded sky.
   - c. engineers who ride on moving sidewalks.

7. Which statement does the article lead you to believe?
   - a. All airports now have subway trains within their gates.
   - b. Engineers are constantly working on the people-moving problem.
   - c. Separate buildings in airports cannot be connected.

8. Why does a small area become crowded in minutes?
   - a. Jet airliners race buses to one small crowded area.
   - b. Crowds rush in to see the air buses and 747s land.
   - c. Thousands of bags and people are unloaded in a short time.

9. Think about the concept for this group of articles. Which statement seems true both for the article and for the concept?
   - a. Moving sidewalks are more practical than trains.
   - b. Airports are too crowded to work well.
   - c. Airports solve their problems in different ways.

A Gift from Holda

Long, long ago, when the Norse gods and goddesses still lived in Asgard (äs' gärd), a shepherd took his flock of sheep up into the mountains. There the sheep could graze on the good, rich grass. And while the sheep grazed, the shepherd could use his bow and arrow to hunt game for his family.

One day, the shepherd was chasing a deer. As the shepherd followed it, he began to climb higher and higher until at last he reached the peak of the mountain. Suddenly the deer disappeared. The shepherd looked about in amazement. Where could the deer have gone? As he searched, he was surprised to see a doorway in a huge boulder. Curious, the shepherd walked through the doorway and into the most spectacular cave he had ever seen in his life.

The cave glittered with precious gems. In the center of the cave stood a beautiful woman dressed in silver. Around her were a group of young girls wearing crowns of roses. The beautiful woman was Holda, goddess of weather. When it rained, people on earth said the goddess Holda was washing her clothes. When it snowed, she was shaking her clothes and bits of clouds were falling. The white clouds were the linens she bleached in the sun. When people saw long strips of gray clouds cross the sky, they said Holda was weaving. Everyone knew that the goddess Holda was a fine spinner and weaver of cloth as well as the guardian of weather. It was Holda who spun and wove cloth for all the gods and goddesses in Asgard. The shepherd did not know that the beautiful woman was Holda. But he thought she might be a powerful goddess. So he just stood rooted to the spot, afraid to move.

"Do not be afraid," the goddess said gently and smiled at the fearful shepherd. "Since you have found this cave, you may take from it anything you choose."

The brilliance of the gems almost blinded the shepherd as he looked around. Wealth beyond his wildest dreams was his for the choosing! But the more he looked at the gems, the more his eyes seemed drawn to a small bouquet of flowers in Holda's hand. At last he said in a timid voice, "Gracious lady, nothing would please me more than the flowers you hold." Holda was very pleased. As she handed the flowers to the shepherd, she said, "Know that you shall live as long as the flowers do not droop or fade." As the shepherd turned to go, the goddess handed him some seeds. "Sow these in your fields," she said. As she spoke, thunder shook the mountain, and lightning flashed through the cave. The shepherd covered his eyes in fright. When he took his hands from his eyes, he found himself at the foot of the mountain. He ran home at once to tell his wife everything that had happened.

"Fool," cried the wife bitterly, when he had finished his story. "You could have had a fortune in gems, and you settled for flowers and seeds?"

The shepherd did not reply, but went at once to sow the seeds. To his amazement, the small handful of seeds was enough to sow several acres of ground. Before long, green shoots began to appear. Shortly after, blue flowers dotted the fields. Then the flowers withered.

"What now?" the wife complained. "We have fields of dying flowers when we might have had precious jewels."

But that night, the goddess Holda came to the shepherd's cottage. She showed the shepherd and his wife how to harvest the stalks of the flowers. Then she taught them to spin and weave and bleach the linen produced from the stalks. It was not long before everyone in the area wanted the beautiful cloth. The linen became so popular that the shepherd spent all his time plowing, sowing, and harvesting. His wife was busy spinning, weaving, and bleaching the linen cloth. Soon the shepherd and his wife were very rich.

So time passed. The shepherd grew very old, old enough to see his great-grandchildren beginning to grow up. One day, the shepherd looked at the bouquet of blue flowers the goddess Holda had given him so long ago in the cave. He saw that the flowers, which had remained fresh all these years, had faded and died. So he knew that he, too, must soon die.

Suddenly he felt a great longing to climb the mountain once more. Slowly, for he was very old, he began the long climb. At last, after many days, he reached the peak of the mountain. He looked about, but his eyes were dim and he could not see. Gently, a hand seemed to lead him to the open doorway in the huge boulder. The shepherd walked through the doorway and was never seen again.

It is said the old man lives there yet, that the goddess Holda protects him and grants him any wish. And all this happened because the timid shepherd chose the simple bouquet rather than the glittering and brilliant jewels in the cave.

841 words

IV

Similar Things Are Changing All Over the World at Different Rates

In this section, you will read about things and ideas that are changing – some rapidly and some slowly. You will read about this in the areas of history, biology, economics, anthropology, geography, Earth science, space, political science, art, and engineering.

Keep these questions in mind when you are reading.

1. Why don't all changes take place at the same time all over the world?

2. What factors determine different rates of change?

3. Do all people want the same amount of change?

4. Should we know about changes taking place in the world? Why?

5. How do changes affect me?

Look on pages 10-12 for help with words you don't understand in this section.

Modern Leaders in Asia

A good Japanese wife always walked several feet behind her husband. She was not considered his equal, and for centuries women did not question this. First the father ruled her, then her husband, and finally, her son.

Since World War II, however, things have changed for Japanese women. Japan's new constitution came into effect in 1946. Women were given the right to vote and to hold public office.

At first, the new laws caused quick change. In 1946, women held more than 7% of the seats in the Japanese Diet, the legislature that makes Japan's laws. But Japanese women soon lost much of their political strength. This changed in the 1980s, when many women were elected to local assemblies. Then in the 1990s, Japanese women began to return to the Diet. In 1996, the number of women there rose from 12 to 23.

Japan is not the only Asian nation in which women have entered the govern-

ment. In 1920, a man named Mahatma Gandhi began the nonviolent campaign against English rule of India. Many women took part in this struggle. Afterward, women remained active in Indian politics. In 1966, Indira Gandhi —who was not related to Mahatma— became India's first woman prime minister. She was prime minister from 1966 to 1977, then from 1980 to 1984.

Other women have also led Asian lands. The first was Sirimavo Bandaranaike, who was elected prime minister of Sri Lanka in 1960. In 1986, Corazon Aquino became president of the Philippines. In 1988, Benazir Bhutto became the prime minister of Pakistan. She was the first woman to lead a Muslim country. In the 1990s, women have been elected to lead Turkey and Bangladesh.

No one can tell what will happen in politics. But the trends suggest that women in Asia will continue to gain political strength.

FIND THE ANSWERS

1. A good Japanese wife walked
   a. behind her husband.
   b. beside her husband.
   c. away from her husband.
   d. in front of her husband.

2. The word in paragraph 1 that means *regarded as* is _____.

3. The words "the first woman to lead a Muslim country" in paragraph 5 describe
   _____ _____.

4. While it is not directly stated, the article suggests that
   a. many women are very interested in politics.
   b. Muslim countries have the most women leaders.
   c. there are no women leaders in modern Japan.

5. The Japanese Diet is
   a. the name for the food in Japan.
   b. Japan's name for its legislature.
   c. the latest Japanese newspaper.

6. On the whole, the article tells about
   a. the way most women vote.
   b. women in government.
   c. India's prime ministers.

7. Which statement does the article lead you to believe?
   a. It is important for women to play an active role in politics.
   b. Women are not interested in their country's future.
   c. Corazon Aquino was the first president of the Philippines.

8. Why does a Japanese wife no longer walk behind her husband?
   a. Japanese no longer marry.
   b. Japanese women have more rights today.
   c. Japanese roads are wider.

9. Think about the concept for this group of articles. Which statement seems true both for the article and for the concept?
   a. Ideas about women have changed in Asia.
   b. The government has changed its mind about nonviolence in India.
   c. Women may no longer vote in Sri Lanka.

MOROCCO

TUNISIA

ALGERIA

The New Flags

The continent of Europe takes up only 8 percent of the world's landmass. Yet at the beginning of the twentieth century, European nations owned great land empires. The colonies they governed were scattered across the globe.

In the early 1900s, the world's largest empire belonged to England, which ruled more than one-quarter of the people on Earth. Its land possessions stretched across the world, and it was said the sun never set on the British Empire. France was the largest colonial power in Africa. France's holdings stretched from north of the Sahara Desert to the tropical rain forests of the Congo. France owned four million square miles of African territory and it governed about 44 million African people. Tiny Holland, whose own land area was little more than 13,000 square miles, was one of the world's leading colonial powers as far back as the seventeenth century. Spain once controlled most of Central and South America.

After World War II, however, colonial empires began to fall apart. Many colonial people would no longer tolerate foreign rulers and were determined to be independent. Over time, more than 40 British colonies became independent. Some French colonies such as Algeria, Morocco, and Tunisia gained full independence. Others became departments of France, which means that they elect representatives to the French Parliament and vote for the president of France. Similarly, the Netherlands Antilles and Aruba became parts of the Netherlands. The other Dutch colonies became independent.

Today, a few countries are still dependent on the once-great colonial empires. But in the past 50 years, whenever a country has wished to become independent, it has usually been able to do so. As a result, more emerging nations are flying their own flags over their own land, and colonial empires are a thing of the past.

1. It was said that the sun never set on
    a. Central America.
    b. the rain forests.
    c. the British Empire.
    d. the Sahara Desert.

2. The word in paragraph 3 that means *put up with* is _____.

3. The words "once controlled most of Central and South America" in paragraph 2 describe the colonial nation _____.

4. While it is not directly stated, the article suggests that
    a. the continent of Europe is now found in Central America.
    b. the continent of Europe takes up all the world's land.
    c. the continent of Europe no longer controls the world.

5. France was the largest colonial power on the continent of
    a. Africa.
    b. America.
    c. Australia.

6. On the whole, the article tells about
    a. the breakdown of colonial empires.
    b. empires that proudly fly flags.
    c. the size of the Sahara Desert.

7. Which statement does the article lead you to believe?
    a. Colonial empires owned land, but had no real power.
    b. Colonial empires are still the best idea for the people.
    c. People no longer accept the idea of colonial empires.

8. Why were European countries great land empires?
    a. They owned land in Central America.
    b. They owned land across the globe.
    c. They governed each other's land.

9. Think about the concept for this group of articles. Which statement seems true both for the article and for the concept?
    a. Small countries do not wish to be free.
    b. Nations should be ruled by outsiders.
    c. Nations around the world want to be free.

The City Moth and the Country Moth

The *Biston betularia* (bis′ tən bet′ ū lãr′ ē ə) is better known in Northern Europe as the peppered moth. It is a very common insect. About a hundred years ago, the peppered moth could be easily identified anywhere by its white wings speckled with tiny black dots. These moths were hard to see against the light-colored lichens and gray bark of trees.

Then industry began to grow. Near Manchester, as in other cities of England, smoke and soot from thousands of chimneys rained down. Factory smoke polluted the air. Black dust coated trees and shrubs.

A strange thing happened to the peppered moth. Peppered moths in Manchester became darker than those that lived in the country. They turned gray. Today, 95 percent of the peppered moths in Manchester are almost black. A similar change was noticed in seventy other species of moths common to Northern Europe.

In an industrial area, a white-winged peppered moth would be quite visible. The dark moths are hard to see against the dark buildings and soot-covered trees. The change from white to almost black coloring gives the peppered moths protection from their enemies.

This color change has not happened in all peppered moths. Insects farther from the center of the industrial area are lighter gray in color. Country moths continue to have white, speckled wings.

Biologists believe that a mutation probably caused the first dark moths. A mutation is a sudden hereditary change. These darker moths were not preyed upon as readily by the birds. More of these darker moths were able to survive in the cities. As a result of the survival of one dark gray generation, other dark generations followed.

1. A mutation is a
   - a. tree with black dust.
   - b. city in North England.
   - c. result of survival.
   - d. sudden hereditary change.

2. The word in paragraph 1 that means *recognized* or *known* is

   _____ .

3. The words "from thousands of chimneys rained down" in paragraph 2

   describe the _____ and _____ .

4. While it is not directly stated, the article suggests that
   - a. the peppered moth is found all over Northern Europe.
   - b. the peppered moth is not a very common insect today.
   - c. the peppered moth pollutes the air in Manchester.

5. A white-winged peppered moth is very visible
   - a. far out in the country.
   - b. in an industrial area.
   - c. against gray bark of trees.

6. On the whole, the article tells about
   - a. industry in the city of Manchester.
   - b. the color of lichens and tree bark.
   - c. the change in some peppered moths.

7. Which statement does the article lead you to believe?
   - a. Country moths love living in the big city.
   - b. Biologists do not believe in insect changes.
   - c. Insects that cannot adapt cannot survive.

8. Why do country moths continue to have white wings?
   - a. They are away from the industrial areas.
   - b. They like white wings better than black ones.
   - c. They want to be easily identified by birds.

9. Think about the concept for this group of articles. Which statement seems true both for the article and for the concept?
   - a. All peppered moths look exactly the same.
   - b. Insects cannot make sudden hereditary changes.
   - c. Insects must adapt to the changes around them.

The Mystery of the Red Tides

What makes the sea turn red and causes thousands of fish to die? As far back as anyone could remember the blame was placed on the "red tides."

In 1947, scientists finally traced the condition called the red tides to a microscopic sea organism called the *dinoflagellate* (di′ nō flaj′ ə lət).

The dinoflagellate is so tiny that 6,000 of these organisms may be contained in a single drop of water. It stands on the borderline between plant and animal in its classification. It manufactures its own food, as plants do. But it moves freely and eats other organisms, as animals do.

Dinoflagellates are normally only one of the many kinds of organisms found in plankton. *Plankton* is the name given to all very small forms of sea life. However, when the air and water are calm and warm, dinoflagellates multiply or "bloom" with amazing speed. The surface of the water appears to be covered with a red carpet.

The "blooming" dinoflagellates give off a poisonous secretion. Many fish die. Their bodies are washed up on the beach. Beaches are not fit for use. Fish that are not killed may become poisonous to animals or people who eat them. Commercial fishing comes to a halt.

As dinoflagellates exhaust the food and oxygen in an area, they die. After a time, the sea returns to normal. But when conditions are right, the red tide blooms again.

At least nine times in this century, the west coast of Florida has been plagued by a red tide. In 1957, the Arabian Sea was affected. At different times, the coasts of western Australia and Peru have suffered from this invasion from the sea.

FIND THE ANSWERS

1. The sea turned red because of the
       a. "red dyes."   c. "red microscope."
       b. "red tides."   d. "red scientists."

2. The word in paragraph 6 that means *use up* is _____.

3. The words "microscopic sea organism" in paragraph 2 describe the

   _____ .

4. While it is not directly stated, the article suggests that
       a. small forms of sea life have no name.
       b. there are many small forms of sea life.
       c. scientists are against all small things.

5. "Blooming" dinoflagellates give off
       a. a carpet covered with blooms.
       b. food and oxygen to fish.
       c. a poisonous secretion.

6. On the whole, the article tells about
       a. the west coast of Florida in 1957.
       b. the real cause of the red tides.
       c. people who eat poisonous fish.

7. Which statement does the article lead you to believe?
       a. Dinoflagellates are too mysterious for scientists.
       b. The mystery of the red tides has been solved.
       c. Someone has been mysteriously poisoning the fish.

8. Why are some beaches not fit for use?
       a. People on the beaches eat the bodies of dead fish.
       b. The bodies of dead fish are washed up on the beaches.
       c. The beaches are covered with animals who eat poison.

9. Think about the concept for this group of articles. Which statement seems true both for the article and for the concept?
       a. It exhausts dinoflagellates to carpet the sea in red.
       b. Many parts of the ocean have had red tides.
       c. People on the West Coast of Florida like red seas.

Feeding the World

Progress in agriculture moves at different rates around the globe. In some places, it moves swiftly. In others, the pace is slow. But everywhere, people look to farmers to provide the necessities of food and clothing.

Since the 1800s, new machines, chemicals, and farming methods have been making farms more and more productive. Now, the farms in western Europe produce the greatest amount of food per acre in the world. Farmers in the United States are also very productive. In this country, an average farmer produces enough food to feed 78 people.

Many countries are still looking for ways to help themselves grow more food. In 1995, the United Nations began helping farmers in Eritrea. These farmers began using fertilizers, new farming techniques, and better seeds. By 1997, many farmers in Eritrea were able to grow two to four times more wheat than before. But experts are still searching for ways to help Eritrea. For example,

because Eritrea gets little rain, scientists are searching for crops that grow quickly and resist droughts.

In northern Uganda, farmers now have a better way to harvest the cassava root, which is their most important crop. Until recently, it took a week to cut, peel, wash, and dry a bitter cassava root. Farmers did this to get rid of a poison called cyanide, which is in the roots. But now, with hand-held tin graters, farmers can make a cassava root safe to eat in just one day. This is an important change, because sometimes people in Uganda are dying of hunger. They cannot wait one week for a cassava root.

The same farming improvements do not help everywhere. Some countries, like Senegal, need irrigation systems to distribute water. Other countries, like Eritrea, need machinery that can process larger amounts of crops at a time. In each place that people are hungry, people will need a different solution.

1. An average farmer in the United States can produce
    a. more than a European farmer.   c. enough food for 78 people.
    b. bitter cassava roots.   d. new farming methods.

2. The word in paragraph 1 that means *needs* is _____.

3. The words "which is their most important crop" in paragraph 4 describe the _____.

4. While it is not directly stated, the article suggests that
    a. the farmer's job is very important.
    b. farmers are not needed anymore.
    c. all farmers use fertilizer.

5. Farmers in western Europe
    a. use hand-held tin graters.
    b. are looking for crops that resist drought.
    c. produce the greatest amount of food per acre.

6. On the whole, the article tells about
    a. new seeds that some farmers use.
    b. rainfall in Eritrea.
    c. how some countries have improved their farming.

7. Which statement does the article lead you to believe?
    a. Farmers have all the machinery they can use today.
    b. People will continue to try new farming methods.
    c. The same farming methods will work everywhere.

8. Why do farmers need to cut, peel, wash, and dry a cassava root?
    a. They need to get rid of poison.
    b. They need to cook the root.
    c. They want to use the outside of the root.

9. Think about the concept for this group of articles. Which statement seems true for both the article and the concept?
    a. Fertilizer will let all countries grow enough food.
    b. Some countries' farmers have made more progress than others.
    c. Most places will never catch up to western Europe.

Networks of Banks

What do villages and big cities have in common? In both, you are sure to find banks. They may be in different kinds of buildings. The amount of business they do may differ greatly. But in both places, banks are important to the community.

Banking goes back to ancient times. In 2000 B.C., Babylonians were charging interest on loans, recording both on clay tablets. In medieval Italy, money lenders conducted their business from *bancas*, or benches, in the streets.

Banks have come a long way from those far-off days. Some small banks still offer limited services. But because of changes in technology, even small banks can offer many new services to their customers.

One of the biggest changes in banking was the invention of the automated teller machine (ATM). An ATM is a computer terminal that people can use to make deposits, to transfer funds, or to withdraw money. ATMs are especially convenient for travelers, because many banks are part of large networks of ATMs. This means that you can use an ATM at a bank that is part of the network, even if it is not your own bank.

Though ATMs were introduced in the United States in the 1970s, they did not become available everywhere at the same time. By the middle of the 1980s most parts of this country had ATMs and networks. In India, Hong Kong, and South Korea, network ATMs became available in the 1990s. But many countries still do not have ATMs.

ATMs vary depending on where they are. In England, a bank decided to make its ATMs friendlier. At these ATMs, customers deal with a teller on a TV screen. In Cleveland, a talking ATM named Bobbie uses motion sensors to tell when people are nearby and greets them.

FIND THE ANSWERS

1. Money lenders conducted their business from
   a. branches.   c. ATMs.
   b. benches.   d. networks.

2. The word in paragraph 5 that means *brought in* is _____.

3. The words "uses motion sensors" in paragraph 6 describe
   _____.

4. While it is not directly stated, the article suggests that
   a. only money lenders use benches.
   b. banks in different places offer different services.
   c. many ATMs can talk.

5. In a network of ATMs, you can use an ATM
   a. only at your bank
   b. at any bank with a video screen.
   c. at any bank that is in the network.

6. On the whole, this story is about
   a. services offered by banks.
   b. banking in India, Hong Kong, and South Korea.
   c. money lenders in the 1980s.

7. Which statement does the article lead you to believe?
   a. Banking services will continue to change.
   b. There are too many ATMs.
   c. The United States will always have the most ATMs.

8. Why did a bank in England begin to use a teller on its video screens?
   a. It wanted to make its ATMs friendlier.
   b. It wanted to make its banks safer.
   c. It wanted its ATMs to use sensors.

9. Think about the concept for this group of articles. Which statement seems true for both the article and the concept?
   a. All banks should have ATMs.
   b. Banking methods change to respond to the needs of the people.
   c. Countries without ATMs do not have enough service.

The Worldwide Fight Against Pollution

In 1952, "killer smog" caused the deaths of more than 4,000 people in London. In 1953 and 1963, weather conditions called thermal inversions, which allow pollution to build up over an area, killed over 600 people in New York City. At the time, few people thought about the pollution that caused these events. But as years passed, more people became interested in keeping our environment clean.

Air pollution has a few main causes. Transportation, such as airplanes and cars, produces exhausts that pollute the air. The furnaces that provide heat release pollutants such as nitrogen oxide and sulfur oxide. Air pollution is also caused by industrial plants, the burning of wastes, chemical sprays, and fires.

Water pollution also has a few different causes. Many industries release toxic chemicals into streams and rivers. Fertilizers from farms and lawns seep into waterways and cause weeds to grow, choking off animal and plant life. The burning of fuels such as oil and coal causes polluted rain called acid rain. Animal waste can also pollute water supplies.

The United States was one of the first countries to set limits on its pollution. Since the 1970s, our government has set goals for reducing air and water pollution. Industries have worked to meet these goals. For example, since 1975, most cars in America have had catalytic converters. Many factories now have scrubbers that remove pollutants before they reach the air.

As time has passed, many countries have decided to work together to fight pollution. In 1989, a group of countries agreed to stop making chemicals called CFCs, which damage our atmosphere. In 1992, representatives of 178 countries held a meeting called the Earth Summit. There, they signed various agreements designed to protect the environment.

Despite this progress, countries are moving at different rates to fight pollution. In some western European countries, there are still problems with exhausts from cars. In some eastern European countries, there are no pollution controls. In China, foreign companies build factories. These plants create pollution that is not permitted in the companies' home countries.

FIND THE ANSWERS

1. "Killer smog" was smog that
   a. was in New York.
   b. was in London.
   c. caused thermal inversion.
   d. was caused by ozone.

2. The word in paragraph 4 that means *making an amount smaller* is

   _____.

3. The words "which damage our atmosphere" in paragraph 5 describe

   _____.

4. While it is not directly stated, the article suggests that
   a   catalytic converters scrub the exhausts from factories.
   b. catalytic converters are no longer used.
   c. catalytic converters cut down on pollution from cars.

5. In some western European countries
   a. there is no problem with water pollution.
   b. foreign companies cause most of the pollution.
   c. there are problems with automobile exhausts.

6. On the whole, the article tells about
   a. meetings between countries.
   b. attempts to reduce water and air pollution.
   c. the burning of wastes.

7. Which statement does the article lead you to believe?
   a. Acid rain creates water pollution.
   b. Acid rain is not a problem in the United States.
   c. We still do not know what causes acid rain.

8. Why did countries agree to stop making CFCs?
   a. CFCs damage our atmosphere.
   b. CFCs damage catalytic converters.
   c. CFCs pollute the water.

9. Think about the concept for this group of articles. Which statement seems true for both the article and the concept?
   a. Some countries have ended all pollution.
   b. The world has agreed on how to control pollution.
   c. Some countries are moving faster than other countries to control pollution.

The Virtual Classroom

Usually, students travel to classrooms. But sometimes schools come to students. All over the world, schools use radio, television, and computers to make "virtual classrooms." These are classrooms made by connecting teachers and students who are in different locations.

The Katherine School of the Air calls itself "the world's largest classroom." It's called that because the Katherine School uses radio to cover 500,000 square miles in Australia's outback country. That's an area twice the size of Texas!

The 275 students of the Katherine School live in remote places such as ranches, mining and fishing camps, and Aboriginal settlements. They are spread far apart and live far away from traditional schools. For these students, classrooms are created by using short-wave radios. These radios provide three-way communication from teacher to child, child to teacher, and child to child. Besides radio lessons, children also work through the mail and by phone.

In other parts of the world, schools use televisions to create "virtual classrooms." In Colorado, National Technological University uses video cameras to connect students to classes at 46 different universities. The cameras and speakerphones let students and professors talk as if they were in the same room.

Some state universities use technology to connect their different locations. In New York, campuses at Binghamton, Buffalo, and Stony Brook use videotapes and computers to create shared classes. In California, two-way video connects campuses.

Some schools use computers to cut class size and to help their students participate in class. Rensselaer Polytechnic Institute once had a physics lecture with 400 students. Now groups of 60 physics students use computers to conduct experiments and answer questions. Drew University students use computers to compose music and to send the music to their teachers.

In the future, more and more schools will use video and computers to connect students and professors who live far away from one another.

FIND THE ANSWERS

1. The Katherine School of the Air uses
   a. video cameras.
   b. computers.
   c. videotapes.
   d. short-wave radios.

2. The word in paragraph 4 that means *school locations* is _____.

3. The words "live in remote places" in paragraph 3 describe the _____ of the Katherine School.

4. While it is not directly stated, the article suggests that
   a. children in Australia cannot be educated.
   b. some children in Australia never see a real classroom.
   c. the outback is a very small area.

5. The National Technological University
   a. uses computers to connect its students and professors
   b. uses cameras to connect its students and professors.
   c. conducts its classes through the mail.

6. On the whole, the article tells about
   a. television of the future.
   b. the teachers in Australia.
   c. different kinds of schools.

7. Which statement does the article lead you to believe?
   a. People all over the world think that education is important.
   b. Computers and televisions do not help schools.
   c. To learn well, students must be in the same room.

8. Why do some schools use television?
   a. People like to watch television.
   b. Television can connect people who are in different places.
   c. Television is the easiest way to learn.

9. Think about the concept for this group of articles. Which statement seems true for both the article and the concept?
   a. The way schools work does not change.
   b. Universities in New York and California have too many students.
   c. Schools are not the same everywhere.

The Flood That Is Welcome

Imagine, if you can, a cubic mile of water. You would have a great liquid block that measured a mile long, a mile wide, and a mile deep. Earth scientists say that about 9,000 cubic miles of water run off the land each year into the seas. This water is only part of the rain that falls yearly. The remainder seeps into the ground or evaporates into the atmosphere.

The world's rainfall is not distributed evenly around the globe. Only about two inches of rain fall in desert areas each year. In jungle regions, there may be 450 inches of rain. On a mountain peak on the island of Kauai (kou'ī) in Hawaii about 480 inches of rain fall yearly. Yet within a few miles of this same area, the rain that falls does not even equal 20 inches a year.

A sudden increase in rainfall can make streams and rivers overflow.

Swirling brown waters may cover areas that are not usually under water. The resulting floods change the shape of the earth.

In some areas of the world, floods are welcome! Along the Nile River in Egypt, floods bring down fertile soil from upstream. In other areas, floods are not welcome, but they are expected. People living along the Mississippi River in the United States or the Yellow River in China know these rivers often overflow their banks. Dikes and levees have been built in these areas to help control floods. In other places, great floods happen so rarely people neither expect them nor are prepared for them. In such unprotected areas, the receding flood waters leave behind great damage. Crops are ruined, homes are destroyed, and the land gets a new shape.

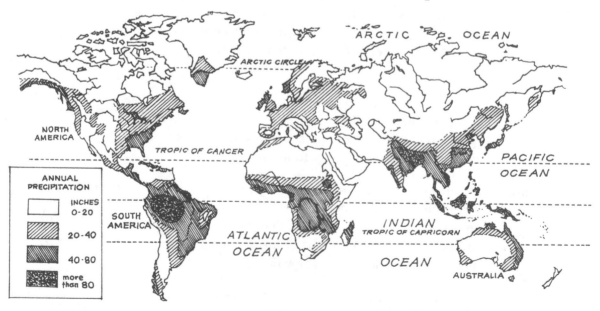

162

1. Floods are welcome in
    a. Egypt.
    b. China.
    c. the United States.
    d. the jungle areas.

2. The word in paragraph 1 that means *flows very slowly* is _____ .

3. The words "change the shape of the earth" in paragraph 3 describe the resulting _____ .

4. While it is not directly stated, the article suggests that
    a. jungle areas do not get much rain.
    b. the land is very dry in some places.
    c. it never rains along the Mississippi.

5. The world's rainfall is not
    a. ever increased at all.
    b. the cause of floods.
    c. distributed evenly.

6. On the whole, the article tells about
    a. the dikes in China.
    b. the Yellow River.
    c. rainfall and floods.

7. Which statement does the article lead you to believe?
    a. It is a good thing for crops to be ruined by floods.
    b. Sometimes the shape of the earth is changed quickly.
    c. It is not possible for floods to change the land.

8. Why are floods welcome along the Nile River?
    a. They bring fertile soil from upstream.
    b. The people like to watch the floods.
    c. It gives the people something to do.

9. Think about the concept for this group of articles. Which statement seems true both for the article and for the concept?
    a. The people in China should not keep building dikes.
    b. Floods do not happen everywhere at the same time.
    c. Floods are always expected everywhere on earth.

What's on TV Tonight?

In 1936, the National Broadcasting Company (NBC) started the first television network. In that year, NBC installed television receivers in 150 homes in the New York City area. Ten years later, a television boom began. By 1960, almost every American home had a television set. But that was just the start. In the years to come, the television industry continued to grow in the United States and in the rest of the world.

In the United States, one of the main things that has changed in television is the number of channels. Until the 1970s, there were only three main television networks. In some areas, there were also a few independent stations or public stations. But in the 1980s, cable networks and satellite networks began to change that. Now, viewers with cable television may have between 40 and 50 channels on their sets. Satellite systems may provide even more channels.

The large number of stations in our country means that we get many kinds of programs. Besides entertainment and sports, there are news and information channels. There are even public access channels on which ordinary people can put their own shows.

Around the world, the number of televisions is still growing, but in many countries, people don't have a wide choice of channels or shows. In 1996, 92 out of 187 world governments owned their country's television networks. Another 67 governments were co-owners of their country's television networks. When a government owns television networks, it can have great control over what people watch. It can limit the information and news that people get. Television can also be used to form opinions. For example, in China, television regularly shows Japan as a dangerous neighbor.

Despite government control, people in many places are slowly getting a wider choice of television shows. In 1994 black South Africans created their own first television network. In the future, people in many different countries may use satellites to receive shows from other places.

1. The first television network was in
   a. South Africa.
   b. China.
   c. the New York City area.
   d. a test station.

2. The word in paragraph 1 that means *put in place* is _____.

3. The words "provide even more channels" in paragraph 2 describe
   _____ _____.

4. While it is not directly stated, the article suggests that
   a. the United States has the widest variety of television shows.
   b. China has the widest variety of television shows.
   c. Television shows are about the same all over the world.

5. Viewers with cable television
   a. can receive only three main television networks.
   b. may have between 40 and 50 channels.
   c. live in 92 different countries.

6. On the whole, the article tells about
   a. how a cable television network works.
   b. the first television network.
   c. television around the world.

7. Which statement does the article lead you to believe?
   a. Some governments keep certain shows off of television.
   b. The television industry in the United States is not growing.
   c. Television does not affect opinions.

8. Why did the number of channels in the United States grow in the 1980s?
   a. Public television stations were added to some areas.
   b. Cable networks and satellite networks offered new channels.
   c. The government stopped controlling television.

9. Think about the concept for this group of articles. Which statement seems true for both the article and the concept?
   a. People around the world do not all receive the same variety of television shows.
   b. Television is the same in most places.
   c. Television use will grow at a slow rate in the future.

The Winds Aloft

Pilots who fly in light planes check with weather stations to learn the direction and velocity of the winds aloft. If necessary, they may estimate that the wind at 3,000 feet is blowing about twice as fast as the wind at the surface. But pilots who fly great airliners at altitudes between six and nine miles high have a different problem.

During World War II, pilots flying B-29 bombers at high altitudes above the Pacific Ocean made startling discoveries. At times, they met head winds so strong that their planes seemed to be standing still. Bombers could not reach their goals and return to their bases on the estimated fuel. Other times, planes might be pushed along by winds as fast as 300 miles an hour. The existence of such strong winds had never before been observed.

Weather scientists studied the pilots' reports. Careful measurements were made of air currents about six miles up, between 30,000 and 40,000 feet. Powerful currents of air generally moving from west to east in the Northern and Southern hemispheres were identified. But the exact position of these great northern winds called the *jet stream* is impossible to chart. The jet stream does not keep to one course. It may change altitudes or move either north or south. Its speeds may go from 100 to 300 miles an hour. In summer, it may turn north. In winter, it is usually swifter, closer to the earth, and nearer to the equator. Little is known of the comparable southern winds.

Pilots of high altitude flights must know the position of the jet stream every hour. By planning courses that make use of the jet stream, pilots save travel time and fuel.

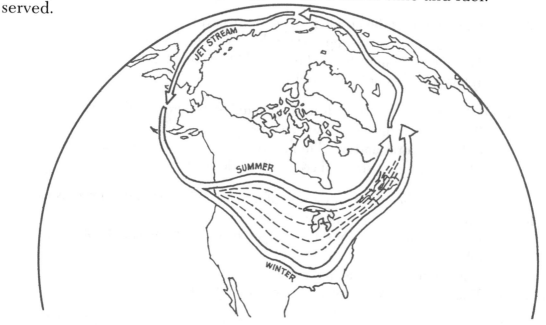

FIND THE ANSWERS

1. The jet stream is known to contain winds of
    a. 30 miles an hour.
    b. 3,000 miles an hour.
    c. 300 miles an hour.
    d. 6 miles an hour.

2. The word in paragraph 1 that means *speed* is _____ .

3. The words "about twice as fast as the wind at the surface" in paragraph 1 describe the _____ at 3,000 feet.

4. While it is not directly stated, the article suggests that
    a. pilots are smarter than all the weather scientists.
    b. many people work together to collect information about our world.
    c. long ago there was no such thing as a jet stream in the world.

5. The great high altitude winds move
    a. generally from east to west.
    b. generally from west to east.
    c. only in a northerly direction.

6. On the whole, the article tells about
    a. the discovery of the jet stream.
    b. high altitude flying.
    c. an invention of weather scientists.

7. Which statement does the article lead you to believe?
    a. A light plane doesn't fly at 30,000 feet.
    b. A light plane and a jet plane are the same.
    c. B-29 bombers also flew in World War I.

8. Why were pilots startled by strong head winds?
    a. The pilots knew strong head winds did not belong so high.
    b. The existence of such strong winds had never been observed.
    c. Weather scientists told the pilots not to look for them.

9. Think about the concept for this group of articles. Which statement seems true both for the article and for the concept?
    a. Winds are the same all over the world in winter and summer.
    b. Nothing is known about wind movements at high altitudes.
    c. People add to their knowledge about winds from time to time.

The Supercontinent

In 1967, two Antarctic explorers dug up some sandstone 325 miles from the South Pole. Deeply imbedded in it was a mysterious fossil. The fossil was part of the jawbone of a labyrinthodont (lab′ ə rin′ thə dont). This animal had lived 200 million years ago. Why was this find so important? The labyrinthodont was a tropical, fresh-water amphibian that had lived in the mud. It could not have reached Antarctica by swimming through the ocean. How had it come to Antarctica?

Fifty years before the fossil was found, Alfred Wegener, a German meteorologist, had stated a surprising theory. He said all the continents of the world had once been combined in one supercontinent. Then this great land mass broke up. North and South America drifted west, and Australia moved south and east. Antarctica traveled toward the South Pole.

Where was Wegener's proof? Scientists asked this again and again. One kind of proof would be to find traces of the same species of animals in Antarctica that had once lived in Africa or Australia. The jawbone of the labyrinthodont was this kind of proof.

Scientists say that the continents are still moving a few inches in many years. This drifting may be caused by pressure beneath the earth's crust. The part of the earth under the crust is called the mantle. The mantle is made up of hot rock materials. In some places it lies less than five miles beneath the surface. The crust is thinnest in the deepest parts of the ocean. Hot material in the mantle might push up and make the floor of the ocean expand. This would push the continents farther away from each other. The movement of the continents is irregular, occurring now in one place and now in another. But no one is really sure what causes it.

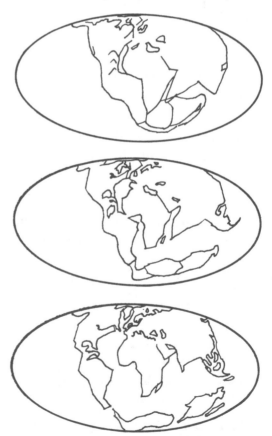

FIND THE ANSWERS

1. Alfred Wegener was a
   a. French explorer.
   b. German meteorologist.
   c. Spanish scientist.
   d. Russian photographer.

2. The word in paragraph 1 that means *firmly and deeply placed* is

   _____ .

3. The words "of hot rock materials" in paragraph 4 describe the

   _____ .

4. While it is not directly stated, the article suggests that
   a. fossils found in Antarctica are not very important today.
   b. scientists cannot tell much from the jawbone of an animal.
   c. the labyrinthodont had lived very far from Antarctica.

5. Scientists say the continents are moving
   a. a few inches in many years.
   b. many feet in just a few months.
   c. ten yards every five minutes.

6. On the whole, the article tells about
   a. animals that lived in Australia.
   b. explorers who live in the South.
   c. the movement of the continents.

7. Which statement does the article lead you to believe?
   a. Scientists always accepted the idea of a supercontinent.
   b. The crust of the earth is the same all around the globe.
   c. Someday the continents may be still farther apart.

8. Why was the Antarctic fossil find so important?
   a. It supported Wegener's theory.
   b. It disproved Wegener's theory.
   c. Alfred Wegener had never found a fossil before.

9. Think about the concept for this group of articles. Which statement seems true both for the article and for the concept?
   a. The continents are not all moving at the same time.
   b. The continents are moving away from each other too fast.
   c. Scientists know that continents can never move at all.

The Exploding Star

Our sun is a star that is about 5 billion years old. It always seems the same to us, but it is changing slowly. It is burning up its own fuel. Hundreds of billions of years from now, it will burn out completely. But meanwhile, it will go on giving off light and heat at a steady rate for about another 5 billion years.

Stars have a "star life." Some of the stars we see are old and burning out. Other stars that will not be visible for centuries are now forming from dust and gases in space.

Early sky watchers called an exploding star a *nova*. Nova is Latin for "new," but exploding stars are not new, just changing. A large star that is blown completely apart when it explodes is called a *supernova* when exploding.

All that remains of one large star that exploded almost 1,000 years ago is a cloud of dust and gases. It is now called the Crab nebula because of its crablike shape. Chinese and Japanese astronomers observed an exploding star from July 4, 1054, to April 17, 1056. They noted the exact place in the sky where this supernova appeared. We believe now that when it exploded, the supernova emitted light 350 million times brighter than the sun. But it was so far away that even when it was brightest, it did not seem as brilliant as the sun to the men who watched it. However, the supernova was so brilliant it could be seen for twenty-three days in broad daylight.

Using modern methods of measurement, today's astronomers know that the explosion which caused the Crab nebula took place exactly as noted by the early astronomers.

The supernova is gone from the sky. But the place it held is still marked today by the expanding cloud of gases and dust we call the Crab nebula.

FIND THE ANSWERS

1. Our sun is
   - a. a supernova.
   - b. gone from the sky.
   - c. burning up its own fuel.
   - d. not giving off any light.

2. The word in paragraph 4 that means *gave off* is _____ .

3. The words "because of its crablike shape" in paragraph 4 describe the

   _____ _____ .

4. While it is not directly stated, the article suggests that
   - a. Chinese astronomers are 1,000 years old.
   - b. Crab nebula is another name for the sun.
   - c. there can be more than one supernova.

5. The Latin word *nova* means
   - a. gas.
   - b. old.
   - c. new.

6. On the whole, the article tells about
   - a. early sky watchers.
   - b. exploding stars.
   - c. the age of the sun.

7. Which statement does the article lead you to believe?
   - a. Exploding stars are always brand new stars.
   - b. Chinese astronomers know more than Japanese do.
   - c. People today can see a nebula that was once a star.

8. Why can astronomers tell the supernova appeared as noted?
   - a. They use modern methods of measurement.
   - b. They are old-fashioned in their ideas.
   - c. The supernova is still bright in the sky.

9. Think about the concept for this group of articles. Which statement seems true both for the article and for the concept?
   - a. Only the Japanese can see supernovas now.
   - b. All stars do not form or die at the same time.
   - c. Supernovas do not give off much light.

Women in Business

1996 was a historic year for women in business. For the first time, each of the top 20 female executives in American companies earned more than $1,000,000. At the top was Linda Wachner, who earned more than $11,000,000. Ms. Wachner, who runs two clothing companies, is also on another list. She's the only woman to head a company on the Fortune 500 list, which is a listing of the nation's 500 largest companies.

For a long time, women have been working to get into business. In this country, Rebecca Lukens was the first woman to head a large company. After her husband died in 1825, Ms. Lukens took over his factory. No one had ever heard of a woman running a steel company! But Ms. Lukens built the factory into a giant company that made iron for railroad cars and equipment. The company, called Lukens Steel, still exists.

Like the steel business, the stock brokerage business has usually been run by men. But in 1870, the sisters Victoria and Tennessee Claf established a stock brokerage in New York. They were helped by Cornelius Vanderbilt, a rich and famous investor.

One of the most famous businesswomen of all time is Mary Kay Ash. In 1963, she started Mary Kay Cosmetics. This company now has subsidiaries in Russia and China. There is even a Mary Kay Museum that has exhibits about the company.

In other countries, women have taken longer to break into business. In Korea, Miky Lee recently became one of the first women to head a big company. Her company manufactures food. In Hong Kong, Joyce Ma runs a chain of stores. Like Ms. Lee, she has helped people in her homeland get used to the idea of a woman running a business.

Women in many countries have made progress in business. But even in the United States, women are still fighting to have an equal opportunity for success. In companies on the Fortune 500 list, women still hold only 2 percent of the top five jobs.

FIND THE ANSWERS

1. Rebecca Lukens ran a
   a. clothing company.
   b. food company.
   c. steel company.
   d. fashion company.

2. The word in paragraph 4 that means *smaller companies that are part of a larger one* is _____.

3. The words "a rich and famous investor" in paragraph 3 describe
   _____ _____.

4. While it is not directly stated, the article suggests that
   a. in Hong Kong, some people did not think women could run a business.
   b. in Korea, no women run businesses.
   c. in Hong Kong, women run most of the businesses.

5. Mary Kay Cosmetics
   a. does business only in the United States.
   b. has subsidiaries in Russia and China.
   c. runs museums all over the world.

6. On the whole, the article tells about
   a. the steel business.
   b. how to start a business.
   c. women in business.

7. Which statement does the article lead you to believe?
   a. Women can run large companies.
   b. Most women are very successful.
   c. Women in Hong Kong will never get ahead.

8. Why did Rebecca Lukens take over a factory?
   a. She was interested in the steel business.
   b. She wanted to build railroad cars.
   c. She wanted to keep the factory going after her husband died.

9. Think about the concept for this group of articles. Which statement seems true for both the article and the concept?
   a. Women prefer to run certain kinds of businesses.
   b. Women are moving ahead in business faster in this country than in other countries.
   c. The United States is the only place where women can work.

George Washington's Warning

What is a political party? It is a group of voters working together to get people of their choice into important government positions. Our major political parties are the Republicans and the Democrats.

Nothing in our Constitution provides for political parties in this country. George Washington even warned the people against forming such groups. But parties developed in spite of his warning. Our first two political parties were the Federalists and the Anti-Federalists. The first group wanted a strong central government. The second group favored strong state governments.

Political parties are not a new idea. There were political parties in ancient Greece and Rome. In England, the first parties were formed in the 1600s, in the time of King Charles II. The Whigs felt the king should serve the government. The Tories believed in the absolute power of the king. Today, the Conservative and Labor parties are England's two major parties.

Here, as in England, the two-party system is strong. Other nations have single parties, three or four parties, or many small parties. Too many small parties can be dangerous. A government may not be able to please so many different groups. When this happens, a dictator may seize control of the country.

Some countries pretend to give their people free elections. But in a dictatorship, there is only one party and one candidate for whom to vote.

Since 1950, more than 40 countries in Africa have become independent. At first, most of these new nations had single ruling parties. But as time has passed, many African nations have set up multi-party democracies. Two of the newest African multi-party systems are in Benin and Zambia.

FIND THE ANSWERS

1. Political parties are
    a. fading away.
    b. very new.
    c. not a new idea.
    d. all the same.

2. The word in paragraph 4 that means *grab* is _____.

3. The words "in the time of King Charles II" in paragraph 3 describe when the first _____ were formed in England.

4. While it is not directly stated, the article suggests that
    a. all countries hold free elections today.
    b. countries do not need political parties.
    c. people have different political ideas.

5. Both Benin and Zambia
    a. are not yet independent.
    b. have single ruling parties.
    c. have multi-party systems.

6. On the whole, the article tells about
    a. different political parties.
    b. the Anti-Federalists in Africa.
    c. Greece and Rome.

7. Which statement does the article lead you to believe?
    a. There are still Tories and Whigs.
    b. George Washington was right.
    c. Political parties are important.

8. Whey are too many small parties dangerous?
    a. They do not let King Charles II rule in England.
    b. They give the people a strong government.
    c. A dictator may seize control of the country.

9. Think about the concept for this group of articles. Which statement seems true both for the article and for the concept?
    a. Political parties hold power at different times.
    b. A dictator can never seize control of a country.
    c. There are no different political parties anywhere.

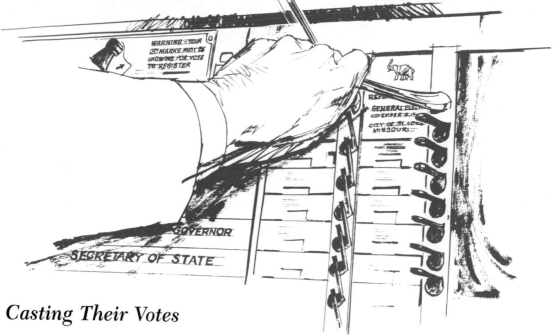

Casting Their Votes

In the United States, some people mark ballots that bear the printed names of candidates. Others pull levers in voting machines. Americans are proud of their long history of holding free elections, but they did not invent the process.

Free elections were held in Athens, Greece, 2,400 years ago. Some Europeans took part in local free elections during the Middle Ages. The secret ballot was first used in 1858 in Australia.

Today, voting is a new experience for many of the world's peoples. Since World War II, many who never had a voice in their government now take part in free elections.

When India held its first national elections in 1951 and 1952, the process was so complicated it took four months. Few people could read, so the ballots bore pictures that stood for the different parties. People who wanted to vote for Gandhi's Congress Party, for example, put an X under the picture of yoked oxen.

In our hemisphere, there are also voters who cannot read. The Dominican Republic, long a dictatorship, held its first free national election in 1962 with rainbow-colored ballots. The different colors identified the parties for people who could not read the candidates' names.

Today, computers are changing the way people vote. In 1994, Mexico set up a computerized voting system. In the future, people all over the world may be able to vote by touching computer screens. These screens could show candidates' names, pictures, or party symbols.

Any change that encourages people to vote helps government work. Oregon lets people vote by mail. Texas has voting in convenient spots such as malls. As long as people want to have a voice in government, they will try new ways of voting.

FIND THE ANSWERS

1. The secret ballot was first used in
   - a. Australia.
   - b. Europe.
   - c. America.
   - d. Athens.

2. The word in paragraph 4 that means *showed* or *carried* is _____.

3. The words "long a dictatorship" in paragraph 5 describe the _____ _____.

4. While it is not directly stated, the article suggests that
   - a. voting is not a good idea.
   - b. there are many ways to vote.
   - c. machines must be used by voters.

5. Rainbow-colored ballots were used in
   - a. the United States.
   - b. Gandhi's Congress Party.
   - c. the Dominican Republic.

6. On the whole, the article tells about
   - a. complicated elections in the Middle Ages.
   - b. the right way to pull a lever in a machine.
   - c. how people vote in many parts of the world.

7. Which statement does the article lead you to believe?
   - a. No one should waste time voting.
   - b. Everyone who can vote should vote.
   - c. Voting is all right for Indonesians.

8. Why did ballots in India bear pictures?
   - a. Few people could read.
   - b. Gandhi liked pictures.
   - c. It made them look pretty.

9. Think about the concept for this group of articles. Which statement seems true both for the article and for the concept?
   - a. People all over the world have been voting for 2,400 years.
   - b. Different peoples got the right to vote at different times.
   - c. Americans invented the process of free elections.

Music for a Haunted House

Quebec, England, France, and Switzerland all played electronic music at the 1967 world's fair, Expo '67, held in Canada. They used it as background music for their exhibits.

What exactly is electronic music? Sounds are produced not on musical instruments but with electronic devices. Electro-magnetic vibrations are changed into sound waves.

Electronic music is not new. It first began to amaze listeners in the early 1900s. They called the new music strange and weird. They said it was music for a haunted house.

Electronic music developed at different rates in different parts of the world. In 1906, an American invented a telharmonium, which made use of alternating electrical currents. In Russia, Leon Theremin, a physicist-musician, invented the boxlike instrument that bears his name. Musicians stand in front of the instrument and wave their hands in the air. Left-hand movements control the loudness of the tone, while right-hand movements raise or lower the pitch.

"Concrete music" was first played in 1948. It was the idea of a French engineer, Pierre Schaeffer. Street noises, radio commercials, conversation, and other sounds were recorded on tapes. The tapes were then run backward. Different kinds of sounds were produced when the speed of the tape was made faster or slower.

In 1955, the electronic synthesizer was invented. Looking something like a cross between a piano and a computer, the synthesizer can produce the entire range of tones that the human ear can hear.

Many people question whether these different sounds are music. Experts say we must get used to new sounds before we can enjoy them. Today, some listeners say they enjoy the new music very much.

FIND THE ANSWERS

1. Concrete music was the idea of
   a. a Russian composer.
   b. a musical expert.
   c. an English physicist.
   d. a French engineer.

2. The word in paragraph 4 that means *taking turns* is _____.

3. The words "for a haunted house" in paragraph 3 describe the strange new _____.

4. While it is not directly stated, the article suggests that
   a. concrete is made from electronic music.
   b. electronic music is a new kind of music.
   c. electronic music has become popular.

5. The theremin is a
   a. musical work.
   b. tape recording.
   c. boxlike device.

6. On the whole, the article tells about
   a. different kinds of electronic music.
   b. a Russian who was a physicist.
   c. people who question the new sounds.

7. Which statement does the article lead you to believe?
   a. New sounds in music can be very interesting.
   b. Electronic music cannot be used for background.
   c. Russian engineers get more ideas than do French engineers.

8. Why was electronic music good for a haunted house?
   a. Unusual sounds could be taped there.
   b. It made vibrations in haunted houses.
   c. The new music was strange and weird.

9. Think about the concept for this group of articles. Which statement seems true both for the article and for the concept?
   a. There was no electronic music at the world's fair in Canada.
   b. Experts say we will never learn to enjoy electronic music.
   c. Many musicians contributed to the development of electronic music.

179

The "Specialty of the House"

There are many different kinds of museums in countries around the world. Many are art museums, where paintings and sculptures may be seen. Some art museums have come to feel that there should not be too many different kinds of art exhibits in the same place at the same time. These museums have begun to limit their exhibits to a specific field.

One New York museum exhibits primitive art only. Viewers can compare New Guinea wood carvings with wood carvings from Kenya, for example. As they move from one carving to another, visitors can learn to understand the meaning of different carvings. They can gain some understanding of the people who made them.

Another museum shows the works of contemporary artists. Often it will exhibit the work of a single artist.

Then visitors can study each painting or sculpture in relation to other works by the same artist. Many other new museums were designed to display the work of a single artist or school. The Lehmbruck Museum in West Germany was built to house only Wilhelm Lehmbruck's sculpture.

In September 1968, the Museum of Modern Art in New York City had a show in which museums themselves were the subjects. From 22 countries, 71 of the newest museums were represented by photographs and models. One new museum decided its specialty would be just magic boxes of all kinds! In America, some art museums make a "specialty" of collections of oriental art. The National Museum of Western Art in Tokyo exhibits only art from the western world.

Today, many people may visit a museum just to see the "specialty of the house."

FIND THE ANSWERS

1. The subjects of a show in the Museum of Modern Art were
   - a. carvings.
   - b. museums.
   - c. oriental art.
   - d. visitors.

2. The word in paragraph 1 that means *displays for the public* is

   _____ .

3. The words "where paintings and sculptures may be seen" in paragraph 1

   refer to the art _____ .

4. While it is not directly stated, the article suggests that
   - a. sculpture is better than paintings.
   - b. people will only look at carvings.
   - c. many people like special exhibits.

5. One new museum decided its specialty would be
   - a. people from New Guinea.
   - b. magic boxes of all kinds.
   - c. an artist who was single.

6. On the whole, the article tells about
   - a. museums with special exhibits.
   - b. the Lehmbruck Museum in Germany.
   - c. all the people who visit museums.

7. Which statement does the article lead you to believe?
   - a. People around the world enjoy art exhibits.
   - b. The Museum of Modern Art is in West Germany.
   - c. Great paintings are no longer found in art museums.

8. Why did some museums limit their exhibits?
   - a. People forced the museums to limit the exhibits.
   - b. They could not get enough exhibits to show people.
   - c. They did not want too many different kinds of art.

9. Think about the concept for this group of articles. Which statement seems true both for the article and for the concept?
   - a. People are not interested in going to museums.
   - b. There are no new museums being built anywhere.
   - c. Not all countries have begun to build "specialty" museums.

Houses of Cardboard?

Suppose someone told you that she was going to buy a house constructed from cardboard and polyester. You might say that she was crazy. Yet, homes like this exist and were designed by a famous architect, Frank Gehry. His homes provide just a few examples of how materials have been used in new ways over the years.

Throughout history, building materials have varied with the resources at hand. Native Americans made teepees of animal skins. The Inuit used sod or snow to build igloos. Adobe bricks made of clay served very well in hot, dry countries.

In recent times, a wide variety of building materials has been available to people all over the world. So, people's choices have been based more on other considerations, such as style or cost. For example, for a long time glass was used only for windows. Then in the 1920s, German designers began to use glass blocks to build walls. This style soon became popular in other countries.

As styles changed, so did the popularity of building materials. Earlier in this century, brick walls inside homes were usually covered by plaster. But in the United States in the 1970s and 1980s, it became popular to show the brick. Many people removed plaster from their inside walls. Homeowners also began showing other features that had been hidden, such as pipes.

For more than 20 years, the architect Frank Gehry has been using materials in new ways. In addition to cardboard and polyester, Gehry has used wire mesh and corrugated metal to build homes. Gehry's work has changed the way people think about building materials. Items that some people thought of as having very little strength are now considered useful building materials!

182

FIND THE ANSWERS

1. Native Americans used animal skins to make
   a. igloos.
   b. teepees.
   c. adobe houses.
   d. glass houses.

2. The word in paragraph 3 that means *different kinds* is _____.

3. The words "covered by plaster" in paragraph 4 describe the _____ _____ inside homes.

4. While it is not directly stated, the article suggests that
   a. there is more than one way to use a building material.
   b. The Inuit will use only adobe bricks in igloos.
   c. Frank Gehry's designs are not popular.

5. In the 1920s, German designers began to
   a. use wire mesh to build walls.
   b. use glass blocks to build walls.
   c. show brick that was inside walls.

6. On the whole, the article tells about
   a. engineers in hot, dry, countries.
   b. how building styles changed in the 1970s.
   c. old and new building materials.

7. Which statement does the article lead you to believe?
   a. People will continue to find new ways to use materials.
   b. Ideas about building do not change.
   c. Frank Gehry's homes are all made from cardboard.

8. Why did some people remove the plaster from their walls?
   a. They thought that plaster was not a safe material.
   b. The plaster did not completely cover the wall.
   c. They wanted to show bricks that were under the plaster.

9. Think about the concept for this group of articles. Which statement seems true for both the article and the concept?
   a. All materials can be used to build homes.
   b. Only in Germany did people use glass blocks.
   c. Our ideas about building materials can come from other countries.

Cooperative Living

What does it mean to live in a cooperative? In some cooperatives, people share only living space. In others, people share work and goals. At different times living in a cooperative has meant different things.

In the 1800s, many Americans formed cooperatives. Some cooperatives had members of just one religious group. Other cooperatives had members of one immigrant group, such as the Swedish. Another American cooperative, called New Harmony, in New York State, was based on the ideas of Robert Owen. He believed that everyone should have equal opportunity. New Harmony had the country's first free library and first trade school.

The most famous American cooperative of the 1800s was Brook Farm in Massachusetts. This place was based on the idea that people with similar interests should live together. Brook Farm was famous because it had many well-known writers and thinkers. Its residents included Ralph Waldo Emerson, Nathaniel Hawthorne, and Margaret Fuller.

Most cooperatives from the 1800s failed, but people kept trying the idea. In Israel, some people live in a kind of cooperative called a kibbutz. These people work together to farm or make products, and to make decisions. The kibbutz uses its profits to take care of its people.

Until 1991, some people in the Soviet Union lived on cooperative farms. Many people think this kind of farm, called a kolkhoz, was not a true cooperative. This is because the government, not the members, had the right to decide what would be done with all food that a kolkhoz produced.

In the 1960s, some young Americans started cooperatives called communes on farms and in cities. Most of these communes failed.

Today in the United States, there are other kinds of cooperatives. In cooperative apartment buildings, people share ownership of the buildings and work together to manage them. Another type of cooperative is a co-housing development. In this kind of cooperative, people work together to design a group of homes for themselves with its own parks and other shared areas.

FIND THE ANSWERS

1. A kibbutz is a kind of cooperative in
   - a. the United States.
   - b. Israel.
   - c. New Harmony.
   - d. Russia.

2. The word in paragraph 3 that means *people who live in a place* is
   _____.

3. The words "most famous American cooperative" in paragraph 3 describe
   _____ _____.

4. While it is not directly stated, the article suggests that
   - a. most cooperatives in Israel have failed.
   - b. all cooperatives have their own libraries.
   - c. New Harmony no longer exists.

5. The cooperative called Brook Farm
   - a. had the country's first trade school.
   - b. had many famous writers and thinkers.
   - c. had members of just one immigrant group.

6. On the whole, the article tells about
   - a. different methods of cooperative farming.
   - b. famous Americans who lived on cooperatives.
   - c. different kinds of cooperatives.

7. Which statement does the article lead you to believe?
   - a. there are still cooperative apartment buildings.
   - b. Brook Farm still exists.
   - c. many communes are found in the United States.

8. Why do some people think that a kolkhoz was not a true cooperative?
   - a. People on a kolkhoz did not share living space.
   - b. The government could decide what to do with a kolkhoz's food.
   - c. People on a kolkhoz did not cooperate.

9. Think about the concept for this group of articles. Which statement seems true for both the article and the concept?
   - a. People are still trying different ways of cooperative living.
   - b. The commune is the only kind of cooperative that has failed.
   - c. Israel and the Soviet Union once had the same kind of cooperatives.

KEEPING CHARTS ON SKILLS

Fill in your record chart after each test. Beside the page numbers, put a one for each correct question. Put zero in the box of each question you missed. At the far right, put your total. Nine is a perfect score for each test.

When you finish all the tests in a concept, total your scores by question. The highest possible score for each question in one concept is the number of stories.

When you have taken several tests, check to see which questions you get right each time. Which ones are you missing? Find the places where you need help. For example, if you are missing Question 3 often, ask for help in learning to use directing words.

As you begin each concept, copy the chart onto lined paper. Down the left side are the test page numbers. Across the top are the question numbers and the kinds of questions. For example, each Question 1 in this book asks you to recall a fact. Your scores for each question show how well you are learning each skill.

Your Reading Scores

Concept II

Question	fact 1	vocabulary 2	modification 3	inference 4	fact 5	main idea 6	inference 7	cause and effect 8	concept recognition 9	Total for Page
Page 59										
61										
63										
65										
67										
69										
71										
73										
75										
77										
79										
81										
83										
85										
87										
89										
91										
93										
95										
97										
Totals by question										

Your Reading Scores

Concept I

Question	fact 1	vocabulary 2	modification 3	inference 4	fact 5	main idea 6	inference 7	cause and effect 8	concept recognition 9	Total for Page
Page 15										
17										
19										
21										
23										
25										
27										
29										
31										
33										
35										
37										
39										
41										
43										
45										
47										
49										
51										
53										
Totals by question										

Question Page	1 fact	2 vocabulary	3 modification	4 inference	5 fact	6 main idea	7 inference	8 cause and effect	9 concept recognition	Total for Page
103										
105										
107										
109										
111										
113										
115										
117										
119										
121										
123										
125										
127										
129										
131										
133										
135										
137										
139										
141										
Totals by question										

Question Page	1 fact	2 vocabulary	3 modification	4 inference	5 fact	6 main idea	7 inference	8 cause and effect	9 concept recognition	Total for Page
147										
149										
151										
153										
155										
157										
159										
161										
163										
165										
167										
169										
171										
173										
175										
177										
179										
181										
183										
185										
Totals by question										